Mozart

HIS LIFE & MUSIC

by Jeremy Siepmann

Author's Acknowledgements

All books are a team effort. This one would not have been possible without the tireless support of my editors Genevieve Helsby and Richard Wigmore, and my wife Deborah, all of whose combination of unwavering standards, imaginative suggestions and inspiring erudition has been both a pleasure and a privilege from the outset. And last, but very far from least, I am indebted to Klaus Heymann, founder and CEO of Naxos Records, who came up with the idea in the first place.

Published by Naxos Books, an imprint of Naxos Rights International Ltd
© Naxos Books 2005
www.naxosbooks.com

Printed in the UK by Biddles Ltd, Norfolk
Design and layout: Hannah Davies, Fruition – Creative Concepts
All photographs © Lebrecht Music & Arts Photo Library
Edited by Richard Wigmore

Title page picture: Portrait of Mozart by J. Lange (his brother-in-law), 1783. Constanze said that this was the best likeness of her husband.
Back cover picture: Mozart as a young man, by Vogel

A CIP Record for this book is available from the British Library.

ISBN: 1-84379-110-2

Contents

www.naxos.com/mozartlifeandmusic

Visit the **dedicated website** for Mozart: His Life & Music and gain free access to the following:

- Many of the works in full which are featured in part on the CDs
- Music by Mozart's father Leopold
- Works by some of Mozart's contemporaries
- A timeline of Mozart's life, set alongside contemporary events in arts, culture and politics
- Special features on particular topics

To access this you will need:

- IBSN: 1843791102
- Password: Amadeus

Preface

The ideal medium for a musical biography has yet to be devised. One essential ingredient on the road to its discovery, however, is the audible presence of the music itself. Notated illustrations are no substitute for the real thing. Only a minority of music lovers today can read a score, much less hear it in their heads, without recourse to an instrument (generally a piano or guitar). To that extent, the invention of the CD has been a godsend to the musical author. Where writers on art and literature have long been able to quote in evidence, printing either the original text or pictorial reproductions, writers on music have had to rely on inadequate verbal description. Then along comes the CD, compact as described, which slips easily into the inside covers, and the problem is solved. In the present case, we have decided to include only whole works, movements or self-contained sections, so that the CDs may be listened to not only in conjunction with the text but purely for pleasure. The hope is that text and music will be mutually nourishing, in whatever mixture.

The book is specifically addressed to a general audience and presumes no formal musical knowledge on the part of the reader. The ratio of biography to musical commentary favours the former by about two to one. Technical terms are explained in the Glossary. The music is not treated in a separate section of the book, as in the conventional life-and-works format, but rather in a sequence of 'Interludes', alternating with the biographical chapters so that readers can, if they wish, opt for a continuous narrative and turn to the specifically musical discussions later on. These musical interludes, in any case, are not analytical. They amount to a generically organised survey of Mozart's colossal output and also include some biographical material. They can be read in any order, but they have been arranged in such a way as to grow naturally out of the narrative chapters that precede them (which are themselves not without musical commentary).

While avoiding the kind of imaginative scene-setting that blights so many biographies, I have attempted to give the book some of the immediacy of a novel by allowing its protagonists wherever possible to relate the story in their own words. These give a far richer and more fascinating portrait of both the characters and their time than any amount of subjective 'interpretation'. That said, interpretation is inevitable: the mere selection of quotations is necessarily an act of interpretation, before commentary even begins. So, in a more passive sense, are the reader's responses to them. There are no absolute truths in biography beyond simple factual accuracy. This book is conceived as no more than an introduction, but it is an introduction to a story without end. No one will ever say all that there is to be said about Mozart. Nor, after more than two centuries, does it look likely that his music will ever lose its power to move, to enchant, to inspire, to console. He is a companion for life.

Prologue: **Mozart in his Time**

The world into which Mozart was born and in which he grew up, matured and died bore little resemblance to the perfect order and pervasive beauty of his music. It was a time of rampant, often violent change, beset by wars and bloody revolutions, none of which he witnessed at first hand, though Salzburg conscripts certainly died in the Seven Years War which broke out in the year of his birth. Social distinctions and political hierarchies which had prevailed for generations were called into question as never before; the structures of wealth and power which had separated the rulers from the ruled were crumbling; and the relationship of church and state, which directly affected Mozart, was tense and potentially volatile. It was small wonder, then, that the musical form which dominated the Classical age of Mozart, Haydn and Beethoven (the so-called sonata form, which they nurtured and brought to its highest state) was fundamentally based on the alternation of stability and flux, and the tension between two different key-centres (see 'Tonality' in the Glossary). Small wonder, too, that sonata form, with its Utopian structure (culminating in the resolution of opposing forces), was an essentially Germanic phenomenon: in the lands controlled by the Habsburg dynasty, unlike in France, the transition into the modern age was effected relatively slowly and peacefully. To this extent Salzburg, however provincial it may have been in other ways, was among the more advanced European cities of the time. In 1764 the Prince-Archbishop Sigismund von Schrattenbach began a series of reforms which were to transform the lives of his subjects, extending in the end to making a colossal donation to the city's communal infirmary, its home for the aged and even its lunatic asylum. A year later, in Vienna (the capital of the Holy Roman Empire of German Lands, to give it its full, cumbersome title), the Empress Maria Theresa and her son Joseph II, who jointly ruled the Empire, embarked on a similar but far more ambitious course. They turned over a large portion of their personal fortune to the civic administrators of the Austrian lands, transferred royal gardens, parks and hunting estates into public ownership, introduced public schooling for the first time, reformed the judicial system (even to the point of rethinking the death penalty), instituted civic marriage, abolished serfdom in Bohemia, encouraged religious tolerance, and so on. This was not democracy, however. The monarchy and the nobility remained firmly in place, but things were not quite what they had been. Partly to keep the numbers up after the ravages of the Seven Years War, and partly to defuse the threat of the rising bourgeoisie (more shrewdly perceived by the Habsburgs than by their French counterparts), first Maria Theresa and then her son adopted the cynical but effective practice of officially ennobling prominent officers, civil servants, industrialists, merchants and businessmen, enriching the ruling nobility by roughly forty new members a year: not so much a case of 'If you can't beat them, join them' as 'If you don't want to be beaten by them, let enough of them join you'. Thus was born a new breed of aristocracy. When 'they' become 'us', so 'we' become stronger. But the royals were playing a dangerous game – and its eventual outcome was to have a decisive effect on Mozart's career, as well as precipitating the end of the Holy Roman Empire within a generation.

If the reforms initiated by Maria Theresa were governed almost entirely by political expediency, those of her son were complicated by a genuine and burning idealism. His reforming zeal galvanised by the death of his mother in 1780, Joseph now carried his egalitarian leanings to the extent of curtailing ceremony in general, cutting back on what he regarded as wasteful expenditure on the more obvious trappings of power and the ostentation of grandiose funerals. He also began mingling freely with the common people. The climate of free thought in Vienna, and its accompanying relaxation of censorship, spawned a degree of intellectual and political debate that became the talk of Europe. Inevitably there would be a backlash. But to Mozart, as a young man lately arrived in the capital, such a climate warranted nothing but optimism, and he counted these years among the happiest of his life.

To his father, it must have seemed almost incredible. When he grew up, as in generations long past, musicians other than wandering minstrels and other such vagabonds were by definition servants, in either an aristocratic or ecclesiastical court (in Mozart's case it was both). They wore servants' livery, just like footmen and coachmen (this applied to Haydn for most of his adult life), and they ate in the servants' kitchen along with the cooks and the scullery maids. Even within the servants' 'household', their status was not high. They were never allowed to travel without their employer's express consent. In some cases (as in Haydn's first post, with the Bohemian Count Morzin) they were even forbidden to marry. Most were expected to double as valets when the need arose (in J.S. Bach's first employment at the court of Weimar he was formally designated as such). Nor had most musicians, even the most gifted, much chance of making it as an independent freelance. Long before Mozart's own travails in that line, Haydn had tried it in Vienna and failed miserably. The gulf between the ruling nobility and the rest of society was vast almost beyond comprehension, and dialogue between them virtually non-existent.

Strange to say, the liberal reforms of Joseph II did little to affect the lot of the court musician. They did, however, help to create a climate in which the gifted composer, particularly if he specialised in Italian opera, could justifiably hope to enjoy a peripatetic career free of bondage to court, church or city. But the risks were still high. Composers never received royalties. Once a work was delivered to the commissioning body, it lay beyond the reach of its creator. Since there were few circumstances in which the original fees could profitably be invested, even the most successful composers were condemned to a hand-to-mouth existence, albeit sometimes at a very high level.

The other road open to the determined freelance was that of the virtuoso performer. It was a role which Mozart fulfilled to perfection for a number of years but which he regarded as a waste of his greatest gift, which was of course for composition. It also involved being almost continuously on the move and was hardly conducive either to composition or to family life, which Mozart cherished. But then, as now, the top performers, especially if they were singers, could command extravagant fees. Indeed a successful singer could make from a single engagement more than twice Mozart's annual salary in Salzburg.

Whichever path he chose, however, Mozart's interests and those of the Emperor were not the same. And in one in particular they were directly opposed. Like the German Pietists a century earlier, although from different motives, the Emperor favoured a radical simplification of music in church. The operatic-style opulence, as he saw it, of music like Mozart's grand masses, was a wasteful and inappropriate extravagance. In 1786 he issued a decree banning 'loud' singing in church. Mozart's career as a composer of church music was over. Only the decidedly unextravagant motet *Ave verum corpus* and the Requiem were to come, both in the last year of his life: the former was written away from Vienna; the latter was intended for the private use of a bereaved nobleman and for a possible subsequent concert performance.

It must be stressed that Joseph's financial and ceremonial economies were not entirely the fruit of his 'enlightened' philosophy. Strictly speaking, the official title of the Holy Roman Empire of German Nations was a bit of euphemistic window-dressing, disguising the fact that it extended far beyond the realm of native German-speakers, embracing (to use another euphemism) significant chunks of Italy, the Netherlands, the Balkans, and all of what we know today as Romania and Hungary. The holding together of such an empire is costly at the best of times. In an age like the latter half of the eighteenth century, rife with political and military unrest, itself intensified by revolutionary and democratic philosophies which threatened the entire social order of a continent, it was very costly indeed. Three times in Mozart's short lifetime (the first in the year of his birth) the outbreak of war resulted in a vast increase in the size of the Emperor's already large standing army (in the War of the Bavarian Succession in 1778–9 it was nearly doubled). In addition to the financial cost of such operations were economic privations. These were felt across the board as skilled craftsmen and many other professionals were drafted into service, and special war taxes, of up to ten per cent, were imposed on state employees, merchants, lawyers, and so on. Farmers and agriculture suffered too, and in 1788 the soaring costs of bread, owing to insufficient grain supplies, reached such heights that there were riots in the streets of Vienna and piratical raids on bakers and granaries.

By that time, the Emperor's brave experiment had begun to backfire on almost every front. The landed nobility had opposed his reforms from the start, rightly fearful of the threat to their wealth and thus their power as well. The proletariat, by far the greatest section of society, had never benefited much from them in the first place. Intellectuals and scholars became disaffected through the increasing neglect of the arts and sciences; and the relaxation of censorship resulted, towards the end of the 1780s, in ever more powerful attacks on the monarchy and its policies by orators and pamphleteers who proved to be gifted manipulators of public opinion. In parts of Hungary and the Netherlands there was open rebellion. With the outbreak of war with Turkey in 1788, and the consequent increases in taxation and enforced recruitment and military expenditure, Joseph's reforms were as good as dead. The clincher came with the eruption of the French Revolution in 1789 and the execution in Paris of Joseph's sister Marie Antoinette, then the Queen of France. Many of his most enlightened laws were repealed, there was a ruthless crackdown on the press, and imprisonment without charge or trial became commonplace. Vienna the bastion of intellectual and artistic freedom disappeared, in the long perspective of history, almost overnight. Alone among the arts, music was relatively unaffected to begin with, though the money to support it became progressively scarcer. Mozart's relations with the Emperor, while never close, remained cordial. But after his appointment as Chamber Composer late in 1787, at a disappointing salary, it had become clear that no further support could be expected from that quarter. By the spring of 1788, opera companies were being disbanded and theatres closed. Despite spiralling debts Mozart, like most freelances before and since, felt it more important than ever to maintain the appearance of prosperity. Accordingly, expenditure began to outrun income, with disastrous effects.

By the time of Joseph's death in 1790, at the age of forty-eight, his 'enlightened' reputation was in ruins and his empire moribund. Nor did the accession of Joseph's brother as Leopold II hold much comfort for Mozart. His hopes of appointment as Second Kapellmeister were soon dashed, and despite his position as court chamber composer he was excluded from the royal retinue at the coronation in Frankfurt in September. Less than two years later, he himself was dead, at the age of thirty-five.

Chapter 1

A Miracle in Salzburg

A Miracle in Salzburg

As the new year dawned in 1756, there was nothing to connect Salzburg with miracles. It was a pretty town, like many other pretty towns, set down like a Christmas ornament in the Austrian plain that surrounded it. With its generous sprinkling of Baroque churches, dominated by the Cathedral of St Ruprecht, it had, then as now, a storybook aura. Its greatest story, however, was still to be told.

Originally a Celtic settlement, later a Roman trading centre, it was established as a bishopric in AD 696 by the Frankish missionary St Rupert and subsequently elevated to the status of archbishopric, with authority over the diocese of Bavaria. Over time, the archbishops became increasingly involved in civic matters, and from the thirteenth century each was granted the title of Prince of the Holy Roman Empire. As autonomous rulers of an imperial city, each kept a musical establishment which served church and city alike. Today, more than 100 churches, castles and palaces bear witness to the power of the Salzburg Prince-Archbishops, music issuing from most of them at one time or another.

It was in 1737 that a seventeen-year-old immigrant from nearby Augsburg in Bavaria flouted the wishes of his parents, who had intended him for the church, and enrolled at Salzburg's university. There he studied logic and jurisprudence. Before graduating, he decided firmly to forsake the church and enter the musical profession. Leopold Mozart was a highly intelligent and cultured man, a very respectable composer, a fine violinist, and eventually the author of an influential treatise on the art of violin playing. For a musician of his time, born just over three decades before the death of J.S. Bach, he was exceptionally well educated. On leaving the university, he joined the musical household of Count Johann Baptist of Thurn-Valsassina and Taxis; three years later he transferred into the service of the Prince-Archbishop (the unmelodiously named Sigismund von Schrattenbach), in which position he was to spend the rest of his life. That, at any rate, had been the intention. In the event, there were some years, to the increasing annoyance of his employer, that he spent well away from the court, hobnobbing with the rich, famous and unimaginably powerful in each of Europe's leading nations, and amassing a small fortune in the process. But this is to anticipate.

In 1747 Leopold Mozart married Maria Anna Pertl. She bore him seven children, of whom only two survived. Given Leopold's insistence that they be brought up on a diet of water and gruel, the wonder is that any survived at all. The elder of the two who did was a daughter, Maria Anna, known as Nannerl to the family. The younger, four and a half years her junior, was Wolfgang Amadeus, born on 27 January 1756. He came by the name of Amadeus only belatedly. In a letter to a friend, Leopold announced his son's name as Joannes Chrisostomos Wolfgangus Gottlieb. When he was christened, a day after his birth (the parents had learned not to take any chances), 'Gottlieb' had given way to 'Theophilus', but Amadeus, the Latinised form of Gottlieb/Theophilus, was nowhere to be seen.

When Wolfgang, cumbrously nicknamed 'Wolfgangerl', was three, Leopold began to teach his sister music. She learned with enthusiasm and astonishing rapidity. Leopold was overjoyed. She had a quick and retentive ear, and took to the keyboard as

3

Entrance to the house of Mozart's birth in Salzburg

naturally as she took to speech. Wolfgang was present at all her lessons, and listened throughout with rapt attention. When Nannerl left off, he would replace her at the keyboard. Almost at once he began to pick out pleasant-sounding intervals: 'thirds' and 'sixths'. The future 'miracle of Salzburg' had already begun to compose. By the time he was four, he could play a number of short pieces faultlessly from memory. Within a year, he was writing them for himself. A family friend, the violinist and court trumpeter Johann Andreas Schachtner, has left us an enchanting account of the composer at the outset of his career:

After one of the Thursday services, I went with Mozart's father to their house, where we found little Wolfgang, then four years old, very busy with his pen. Said his father: 'What are you doing?' Wolfgang replied, 'I am writing a concerto for the clavier; it will soon be done.' 'Let me see it,' said his father. 'It's not finished yet.' 'Never mind; let me see it. It must be something very fine.' His father took it from him and showed me a daub of notes, for the most part written over ink blots. (The little fellow dipped his pen every time down to the very bottom of the ink bottle, so that as soon as it reached the paper, down fell a blot. That did not disturb him in the least. He rubbed the palm of his hand over it, wiped it off, and went on with his writing.) We laughed at first at this apparent nonsense, but then his father began to take in the theme, the notes, the composition; his contemplation of the page became more earnest, and at last tears of wonder and delight fell from his eyes. 'Look, Herr Schachtner! How correct and how orderly it is!

Only it could never be of any use, for it is so extraordinarily difficult that no one in the world could play it.' Then Wolfgang struck in: 'That's why it's a concerto; it must be practised till it's perfect.' He began to play, but could bring out only enough to show us what he meant by it. He had at that time a firm conviction that playing concertos and working miracles were one and the same!

Mozart the composer, however, lagged some way behind Mozart the player. We have it on good authority that on 24 January 1761, three days before his fifth birthday, he learned a scherzo by Georg Christoph Wagenseil between nine and nine-thirty in the evening – an unusual time for a small child to be practising, especially in an age without electric light. On 1 September in the same year, he made his debut as a performer, at the University of Salzburg. By this time his father could barely contain his excitement. He now had not one but two prodigies in the family. By the time she was ten, it was generally agreed that Nannerl could outshine most professional keyboard players three times her age: a prodigy indeed. To Wolfgang, however, Leopold ascribed another word, which was to be echoed through the centuries.

Our most gracious Prince does not, like some, see fit to dispatch liars, cheats and mountebanks abroad, to throw dust in the eyes of the populace. No, he sends good, upright citizens to proclaim to the world a miracle! – ordained by Almighty God, in the town of Salzburg. And if ever it is to be my humble obligation to convince the world of this miracle, that time is now, when people mock the very concept and truth of miracles. They must now be convinced of their folly.

If the world would not hasten to the manger, then he would take the manger to the world. In the course of the next ten years or so, Wolfgang, in the almost constant presence of his father, undertook a series of lengthy and gruelling tours which would have defeated most adults. They started gently enough, however. In January 1762, Leopold, leaving his wife at home, took the two wonder children to Munich, where they played for and presumably astonished the Elector Maximilian III. Strangely, since Leopold was an almost compulsive correspondent, there are no letters giving any details of the visit. All we know is that it took three weeks and that it marked the children's first glimpse of life at court. The Prince-Archbishop of Salzburg, it appears, had not shown sufficient interest in the marvels on his doorstep to invite them in. This is both odd and significant, not merely because Leopold was his employee but because the children were what

Mozart, aged 6

today would be seen as a publicist's dream, potentially the brightest jewels in Salzburg's crown – a thought which seems not to have crossed the Prince-Archbishop's mind. In any case, he gave his blessing to another, longer tour, which kept the whole family away from Salzburg for a little under four months. Despite his tendency to self-importance, it seems that Leopold's services were more easily dispensed with than he might have liked.

Their destination this time was the Imperial Court at Vienna, where the children were to become the darlings of the nobility and aristocracy from the Emperor downwards. In the course of a journey which lasted fully three weeks, there were important stops to be made along the way. With every one, the fame of the children grew, spreading out like ripples in a pond. They stayed for six days in Passau and nine in Linz, playing for the nobility in each, and the children could hardly have been happier. 'They are as cheerful as can be imagined,' wrote Leopold. 'Wherever we go, they behave precisely as they do at home. The boy is so friendly and natural with strangers, and particularly the officers, that you would think they had been lifelong friends.' In addition to his native charm, Wolfgang seemed gifted with all the instincts of a diplomat – a fact which paid some unexpected dividends. As Leopold reported to their landlord back in Salzburg:

> We managed to bypass customs altogether, thanks entirely to little Wolfgang, who instantly befriended the officer on duty, showing off his clavier, playing a minuet on his little fiddle, and then inviting the fellow to call on us. The customs officer accepted his kind offer and took down our address for that very purpose. And that's all there was to it. We were through!

Wherever they went, it was the same story. Wolfgang turned all heads:

> At noon on Tuesday we reached the town of Ybbs, where two friars whom we had met on the boat said Masses – in the course of which our Wolfgang went to the organ and played so brilliantly that the resident Franciscans, who were lunching with guests, abandoned their meal at once and rushed to the choir loft, where they almost expired with astonishment.

By the time the Mozarts reached Vienna and made their command appearance at the great palace of Schönbrunn, their reputations had preceded them, and they were in almost every sense royally received.

Their Majesties treated us so graciously that you'd have thought we were royalty ourselves. Wolfgang enchanted the whole company, especially when he leapt up onto the lap of the Empress, hugged her round the neck and gave her a great kiss. We were there for most of the afternoon and at one point the Emperor himself invited me to hear the little princess play on her violin. On the 15th the Privy Paymaster, on the express instruction of the Empress herself, arrived at our door to present us with two dresses, one for Wolfgang, the other for Nannerl. As soon as we receive the official command, the children are to appear at court and the Privy Paymaster will fetch them. Today at half past two they shall be taken to meet, firstly, the two youngest Archdukes and then at four o'clock, the Hungarian Chancellor, Count Paiffy. Yesterday we were entertained by Count Kaunitz, the day before that we were with Countess Kinsky and later with Count von Ulefeld. And we have still more engagements tomorrow and the day after.

In time to come they would fit a similar number of engagements into a single day. Yet neither child ever complained of fatigue or a disinclination to do what was expected of them.

So much is made – was made at the time – of Mozart's genius that we too easily lose sight of the child behind it. To those outside his intimate family circle he presented an image that only deepened his appeal, and lived for a long time in the memories of those who experienced it at first hand. The Baron Friedrich Melchior von Grimm, for instance, was captivated like virtually everyone else:

He is one of the most enchanting children one could ever hope to meet: whatever he says, whatever he does, brims over with the greatest vitality and spirit, combined with the innocent charm and sweetness of his tender years. His utterly unforced cheerfulness even rids one of the fear that he may burn out before achieving his full maturity.

The cheerfulness was genuine, but it was only a part of the whole picture. Despite the enormous fuss that was made over him for almost as long as he could remember, Mozart seems to have craved affection to a degree that suggests a real insecurity, as though he was fearful of being loved for what he did rather than for what he was – a common experience of prodigies to this day. The anxiety was as real as the cheerfulness. It haunted him to the end of his days, and brought him much unhappiness. It was something his sister glimpsed but never really understood, as she recalled him shortly after his death:

> *He was so extremely fond of me – I, of course fairly doting upon him – that he would repeatedly enquire whether I truly loved him; and when in jest I would occasionally say 'No', his little eyes would fill with tears, so sensitive and loving was his heart.*

Others told a similar story. As with most children, his early love was greatest, though not perhaps healthiest, within his family:

> *He loved our parents, especially our father, so much that he composed a little tune which he would sing every night before going to bed – for which purpose our father would stand him on a chair. Father was invariably required to sing the second part, and when this little ritual, which was never overlooked, was finished, Wolfgang would kiss our father very sweetly and go to sleep peaceful and contented. And this went on, every night, except when he was ill and already in bed, until he was in his tenth year.*

It was in that year, too, that Mozart shed one of his most abiding childhood fears. As Johann Schachtner recalled:

> *Until he was almost ten years old, he had an insurmountable horror of the trumpet when it was sounded alone, without other*

instruments; merely holding a trumpet toward him terrified him as much as if it had been a loaded pistol. His father wished to overcome this childish alarm, and ordered me once, in spite of the boy's pathetic pleading, to blow towards him; but, oh God! how I wish that I had not been induced to do it. Wolfgang no sooner heard the blaring sound than he turned deathly pale, began to collapse, and would certainly have fallen into convulsions, had I not immediately left off.

In such reminiscences we begin to see the darker side of Leopold as parent. This did not lighten as time went on.

As Mozart could not have known, the trumpet, in every society in the world, was (and in many places remains) a powerfully male, even phallic symbol: penetrating, aggressive, authoritarian and intimidating. Not for nothing is the trumpet almost universally a military instrument, designed to rally the troops and frighten the enemy. In eighteenth-century European music, particularly in the Baroque era, it was also the pre-eminent instrument for celebrating the glory of God. Could there be a connection between Mozart's fear of the trumpet and a fear of his father? His childhood motto, which he still occasionally invoked in adult life, usually in times of stress, was 'After God, Papa'. And like God, Papa was the one who gave and who withheld. It was one of his principal teaching techniques. Significantly, he was Mozart's only teacher (neither of the children ever went to school, and they were thus raised largely deprived of friendships with their contemporaries).

Love, fear and even hatred are often intertwined. The love and fear of his father was one of the most powerful features of Mozart's personality, and the engine which shaped his worldly life as he grew into manhood. Of course, these are big issues, which can never be wholly resolved. It may, however, be no coincidence that Mozart overcame his fear of the trumpet in the same year as he abandoned the ritual bedtime song with his father – a ritual probably designed, subconsciously, to ward off any paternal displeasure at the end of the day and give himself the chance of a peaceful night's sleep. In the years of these early tours, his fears were as evident to those close to him as his gaiety was to the public. Often he would remember friends left behind in Salzburg, and cry because he feared he might never see them again. And like all imaginative and sensitive children, as Nannerl observed, he had a rich vein of fantasy:

> He created an entire imaginary kingdom in the course of our travels, which he called the Kingdom of Back – I can't remember why. This kingdom and those who dwelt in it were blessed with everything that could make them good and happy children. He himself was the King – and he carried this charming fantasy so far that our servant, who was rather good at drawing, had to make a map of the entire kingdom, with Wolfgang dictating to him the names of all the cities, market towns and villages.

Interestingly, this ideal kingdom consisted entirely of children. Or to put it more pointedly, it contained no adults. In the long tours which dominated his childhood, Mozart's days were spent almost exclusively amongst adults and, as it must often have seemed, solely for the benefit of adults   Leopold above all. He was not, however, a morbid child. As old Schachtner recalled, his sense of fun was a major part of his personality from infancy to death.

> As soon as he began to give himself up to music, his mind was as good as dead to all other concerns, and even his childish games and toys had to be accompanied by music. When we, that is, he and I, carried his toys from one room into another, for instance, the one of us who went empty-handed had always to sing a march

11

and play the fiddle. But before he began to study music he was so keenly alive to any childish fun that contained a spice of mischief, that even his meals would be forgotten for it.

That spirit of mischief never left him. Many years later, in 1787, it surfaced in his merciless parody of bad composers, *A Musical Joke*. Taken at face value, the work is amusing enough – most amusing when least obvious – but the spectacle of a supreme genius at the height of his powers mocking those less blessed with talent than himself is not a pleasant one. The mischief has been contaminated by malice. Of that there was no sign in the child.

Twenty-five years earlier, in 1762, after a week of playing almost daily for the Imperial Court of Vienna, Wolfgang fell ill with scarlet fever. By that time the royal family and other members of the nobility had showered the Mozarts with money, jewellery and expensive clothing, and Leopold had sent back to Salzburg, to be put in the bank, money equivalent to more than two years of his salary there. After a lifetime of scrimping and saving, he and his wife now realised beyond any shadow of a doubt that their children (and Wolfgang in particular) were their ticket to fame and fortune. The scarlet fever was unfortunate. It kept Mozart bedridden and often in pain for two weeks. Leopold was concerned, of course, but not entirely for his son. As he could not help himself from noting, 'This affair has cost me *fifty ducats at least.*' By the end of December the novelty value of the Mozart enterprise had become somewhat tarnished in Vienna, and it was time, in any case, to head for home.

Interlude I:
The Prodigy Phenomenon

In 1954, a young English doctor and athlete, Roger Bannister, attracted the attention of the world by breaking the hitherto insurmountable barrier of the four-minute mile. Within two months, an Australian, John Landy, had equalled his achievement, and then Bannister broke his own earlier record. From that time on, the sub-four-minute mile became almost a commonplace. In the previous year, Tenzing Norgay and Edmund Hillary had captured the Holy Grail of mountaineers when they reached the summit of Mount Everest. Since then, the summit has become something just short of a glorified picnic site, and the mountainside is strewn with litter. Time and again the once-unachievable has become almost routine.

In the realm of music, the high-pressure marketing of child prodigies started with Mozart (and, coincidentally, with the rise of the piano). Of earlier prodigies, though there were some, we know next to nothing. After Mozart they proliferated like the proverbial rabbits, though more variously. Thus in 1791, the year of Mozart's death, we find a certain 'Miss Hoffmann', aged six, performing concertos on the piano and the harp, assisted on the kettledrum by her brother, who had at that time advanced to the imposing age of three and a half. In Italy, and later England, there was Muzio Clementi, an altogether more serious proposition, who became a highly successful composer and one of the first real

13

piano virtuosos. In Spain, there was Juan Crisóstomo Arriaga, whose precocity by the time he reached the age of twelve was comparable to that of Mozart (it would be easy to mistake his music for Rossini's) but who died before he reached the age of twenty. In Germany, Felix Mendelssohn was an astonishing prodigy, and more multi-faceted than Mozart, but was spared exploitation by his enlightened family. At the age of eight, he could play all Beethoven's symphonies on the piano from memory except for the Ninth (which had not yet been written). When it came to playing the piano, Liszt at ten was probably streets ahead of Mozart at the same age, and at twelve he was no mean composer. Camille Saint-Saëns was playing and composing at three. When at the age of ten he made his official recital debut, he reputedly offered to play as an encore any of Beethoven's thirty-two piano sonatas (this beggars belief). Much later in the century came the astounding Mieczysław Horszowski, who became, among other things, one of the greatest Mozart players who ever lived. At three, though not yet able to read music, he played some of Mendelssohn's *Songs without Words*, and at five he could not only play all of Bach's two- and three-part inventions from memory but transpose them into any key at a moment's notice. He was also able to take down in dictation anything he heard, no matter how complex, and had embarked on his own (short-lived) composing career with a number of piano pieces, including two sonatas and a meticulously scored work for full symphony orchestra. At the time of his retirement at 100, he had had a performing career of ninety-five years!

Of the great twentieth-century virtuosos, most (including Vladimir Ashkenazy, Claudio Arrau, Martha Argerich, Daniel Barenboim, Shura Cherkassky, Josef Hofmann, Vladimir Horowitz, Julius Katchen, Dinu Lipatti, Guiomar Novaës, John Ogdon, Rudolf and Peter Serkin, Artur Rubinstein and Solomon) were seasoned performers, and in some cases worldwide celebrities, before they reached their teens. None was more prodigiously gifted, however, than the Romanian pianist Clara Haskil, who returned from a piano recital at the age of five and played the entire programme, note perfect, without ever having had a piano lesson. Unlike many other prodigies, she retained this talent till the end of her life, and was able to perform a wide repertoire of notoriously difficult virtuoso works without ever having seen them before.

One of the most extraordinary things about all these 'wonder children', however, is that one looks almost in vain for their counterparts in other fields. The only possible exceptions are chess and mathematics, the latter having many affinities with music. The French theologian and scientist Blaise Pascal secretly devised a geometry of his own, aged eleven, and the American mathematician Norbert Wiener was widely read in science and literature at five, entering university six years later. Among the great names in chess are the Ukrainian Sergei Karjakin (at twelve, the youngest grandmaster ever), the Norwegian Magnus Carlsen, and the Russian-American Samuel Reshevsky, who learned to play at the age of four and was beating established adult players with ease at the age of eight.

But where are their equivalents in the realms of literature, painting and theatre? True, the great German artist Albrecht Dürer (1471–1528) was painting creditable self-portraits at thirteen, but these were hardly comparable to the symphonies of Mozart and Mendelssohn at the same age. There has been the odd clutch of precocious writers too, but, again, on nothing like the scale that one finds in music. Why music, the writing and playing of which are among the most contrived and unnatural of human achievements, should be so favoured with childhood geniuses is a question never satisfactorily answered. Let us simply be grateful that few if any musical children have matched the career of the eighteenth-century German, Christian Heinecken.

Fluent in Latin, Greek and French at the age of three, and with a proven and formidable knowledge of history, geography and biblical studies, Master Heinecken breathed his last in 1725, at the tender age of five.

The point about all of these, in the present context, is that the achievement of each, as a performer, was in all likelihood at least the equal of Mozart's at the same age. In one sense, their achievement was still more spectacular, since each new generation had a progressively vaster well of repertoire on which to draw.

With the simultaneous blossoming of musicological scholarship and electronics in the twentieth century, we were given the keys to a musical treasure house which Mozart could never have dreamed of. We have available to us, in score and in sound, the music of thousands of composers, and at the touch of a button. As the twenty-first century develops, even that button may become obsolete. We have not only the music but also books, articles, broadcasts and recordings that can tell us just how it would have been played in the time and place of composition. We have a huge range of authentic instruments going back several centuries, and have learned how to play them as expertly as the finest executants of their particular period. In the context of our present historical awareness, the music of Bach, Handel and Vivaldi seems comparatively recent.

We take it for granted. Mozart had none of this. Even at the time of his death, the names of Byrd, Frescobaldi and Monteverdi were almost certainly unknown to him. Hard though it may be to credit, it was not until the 1780s, when he was at the height of his powers, that he discovered the works of Bach and Handel. Among the fruits of those encounters are Mozart's only keyboard suite, his Prelude and Fugue in C for keyboard, his arrangements for string trio of Bach fugues, preceded by preludes of his own, and his fascinating orchestration of Handel's *Messiah*. Yet their music played no part in his upbringing. As a composer, Bach had been eclipsed by his sons Carl Philipp Emanuel and Johann Christian, and was widely regarded, by those who regarded him at all, as something of an academic fuddy-duddy. His eclipse, though, was not only due to his sons but to the temper of the times. In 1753, only three years after J.S. Bach's death, he and his like were dispatched by the French philosopher-musician Jean-Jacques Rousseau with stupefying arrogance:

> *Fugues, imitations, double designs, and all complex contrapuntal structures... these are arbitrary and purely conventional devices which have hardly any merit save that of a difficulty overcome – difficult sillinesses which the ear cannot endure and reason cannot justify. They are evidently the remains of barbarism and bad taste, that only persist, like the portals of our Gothic churches, to the shame of those who have had the patience to construct them.*
>
> (Lettre sur la Musique Française, 1753)

Few would have put it quite like that, but many shared Rousseau's opinion. Not only Bach but an entire epoch was largely swept aside. The expressive interweaving of multiple melodic strands gave way to the simpler texture of melody and accompaniment. This trend had everything to do with the rise of a market-orientated middle class. Unversed in the traditional musical expertise of the ruling classes, the emergent bourgeoisie had a hunger for music that was fuelled in part by social ambition. By imitating the aristocracy, so the reasoning went, they themselves would be exalted – a case not so much of keeping up with the Joneses as of keeping ahead of them. The increasing demand for simplicity and pleasant tunefulness went hand-in-glove with an increasingly general triviality. 'Dumbing down' was not born yesterday. Nor, however, was it all-pervasive. At the court of provincial Salzburg in Mozart's earliest years, his father (German, not Austrian, in background and training, and a natural conservative) regarded many of his colleagues in the musical household with a contempt he did little to conceal.

What, then, did Mozart hear as a small child? The best probably came from C.P.E. and J.C. Bach, but they were the spices in a diet typified by such minor figures as Eckard, Gassmann, Michael Haydn (remembered until relatively recently only as the hard-drinking brother of Joseph), Honauer, Raupach, Reutter, Schobert (not to be confused with Schubert), Wagenseil – and, yes, Leopold Mozart. As their names imply, they were all German or Austrian, none of them (with the exception of the two Bachs and possibly Michael Haydn) much more than footnotes in musical history. Italian music played almost no part in the child Mozart's earliest development, partly because it was almost exclusively operatic (Salzburg had no opera theatre), but also because it was in a major slump. Its most famous star in German-speaking lands at that time was Niccolò Jommelli, an excellent musician whose name and music were both largely forgotten a generation after his death.

If we can say with some certainty what kind of music Mozart would have heard in his first five years, we remain almost completely in the dark as to what music he actually played. Contemporary accounts are confined exclusively to descriptions of his playing and its effect on all who heard it. This is doubly surprising since his career as a composer began when he was five. Surely he must have played at least some of his own pieces, yet, strange to say, nobody mentions it.

Chapter 2

The Grand Tour

The Grand Tour

Once back in Salzburg, Mozart, still some way short of his seventh birthday, almost immediately fell ill again, this time with rheumatic fever. No sooner had he recovered than he sprang a surprise which left his father speechless. Johann Schachtner, too, was present:

> There came to the house one day our excellent violinist, the late Herr Wenzel, who was a dabbler in composition. He brought six new trios with him, of which he had come to ask our opinion. We played these trios, Mozart's father taking the bass part, Wenzel playing first violin, and I second. Wolfgang then appeared, carrying a little violin which had been given to him in Vienna, and begged to be allowed to play second violin, but his father scolded him for so silly a request, since he had never had any instruction on the violin, and his father thought he was not in the least capable of playing. Wolfgang said, 'One need not have learned, in order to play second violin,' whereupon his father told him to go away at once, and not interrupt us any further. Wolfgang began to cry bitterly, and slunk away with his little violin. I interceded for him to be allowed to play with me, and at last his father said: 'Alright, play with Herr Schachtner then, but not so as to be heard, or you must leave us at once.' So it was settled, and Wolfgang played with me. I soon realised with astonishment that I was quite

superfluous; I put my violin quietly down, and looked at his father,
down whose cheeks tears of wonder and delight were running; and
so he played all six trios.

This was an unexpected turn, to say the least. Well before reaching his teens, Mozart rivalled his father on the violin and looked set to become, in Leopold's own words, 'one of the finest violinists in all Europe'.

Six months after their return to Salzburg from Vienna, the Mozarts were off again, not, this time, for a matter of months but for three and a half years. They visited all the chief towns and cities of southern Germany and the Rhineland, spent a few weeks in Brussels, the first winter in Paris, almost a year and a half in London, the winter of 1765–6 in Holland, finally making their way back to Salzburg by way of Paris, Geneva, Berne and Munich. It was a period of heady triumphs, mounting homesickness for Maria Anna, and episodes of serious illness for all, especially the children, who more than once came close to death. Even in times of good health, the circumstances can only have added to the confusion and anxieties of Nannerl, who passed from girlhood to womanhood in the course of the tour. To add to the physical and psychological strains of the transition, with every passing month and year she moved closer to the periphery of the Mozartian road show. While Nannerl perceptibly grew older, Leopold, aware that time was not on their side, lowered Wolfgang's age by a year for much of the tour, so that he miraculously remained seven for two years running. So much else about him was truly miraculous that no one seemed to notice, or if they did they were past caring. From the reports of the German Baron Friedrich Melchior von Grimm, a diplomat and much admired author, long resident in Paris, it seems that Leopold was trying to strike a delicate balance between true art and the tawdry values of a circus freak show. Grimm also observed, revealingly, 'The father is a respectable, sensible man of

Leopold Mozart with his children, Wolfgang Amadeus and Maria Anna ('Nannerl'), in Paris, 1763; by Louis de Carmontelle

considerable intelligence – and never have I seen a musician who combined his natural talent with such an amazing knack for raking in the money!'

In England Leopold outdid himself. Not content with courting (and conquering) the King and Queen and the cream of the aristocracy, he went for the most gullible of the middle class and shamelessly appealed to the rabble of the pubs and taverns. One so-called 'concert' announcement proclaimed that, in addition to his astounding keyboard virtuosity:

The boy will also play a concerto on the violin, accompany symphonies on the clavier, completely cover the manual or keyboard of the clavier, and play on the cloth as well as though he had the keyboard under his eyes; he will further most accurately name from a distance any notes that may be sounded for him either singly or in chords, on the clavier or on every imaginable instrument including bells, glasses and clocks. Lastly, he will improvise out of his head, not only on the pianoforte but also on the organ.

The cloth-over-the-keys stunt became a staple of the sideshow. The fact is, though, that any proficient pianist could do it, and a blind pianist would have no trouble at all. Curiously enough, it rates not a mention in the bizarre and ungrammatical announcement for a concert on 5 June 1764:

Miss Mozart of eleven and Master Mozart of seven Years of Age, Prodigies of Nature; taking the opportunity of representing to the Public the greatest Prodigy that Europe or that Human Nature has to boast of. Every Body will be astonished to hear a Child of such tender Age playing the Harpsichord in such a Perfection – it surmounts all possible Fantastic and Imagination, and it is hard to express which is more astonishing, his Execution upon the Harpsichord, playing at Sight, or his own Composition.

Journey 1: 1763–6

Present-day international boundaries are shown

AMSTERDAM
THE HAGUE
ANTWERP
MAINZ, FRANKFURT
LILLE
LONDON 13
GHENT
KOBLENZ
SCHWETZINGEN, HEIDELBERG
17 19 18
16 14
15
11
10 9 8
LUDWIGSBURG
BONN 7
BRUSSELS
AUGSBURG
6
MUNICH
AIX-LA-CHAPELLE
5
NYMPHENBURG
4 25
12
3 2
1, 26
PARIS 20
24
SALZBURG
23
WASSERBURG
22 ZÜRICH
21
BERNE
GENEVA
DONAUESCHINGEN

Origin: Salzburg (**1**)

1763

Wasserburg (**2**)	Wolfgang (7) encounters a pedal organ for the first time.
Nymphenburg (**3**)	He plays both harpsichord and violin for the Elector of Bavaria.
Augsburg (**4**)	The children give three concerts during their two-week stay.
Ludwigsburg (**5**)	Typically, Leopold suspects a plot when Duke Karl Eugen of Württemberg declines to hear the children play.
Schwetzingen (**6**)	The Elector Palatine Carl Theodor arranges a four-hour concert by the children, including the participation of the famous Mannheim orchestra.
Heidelberg (**6**)	Wolfgang astounds all present when he plays the organ at the Church of the Holy Ghost.
Mainz (**7**)	The children give two concerts and bring in 200 florins, much to Leopold's satisfaction.
Frankfurt (**7**)	The children give four concerts, one in the presence of the fourteen year old Goethe, who later recalled 'the little man with wig and sword'. The last concert, given by Wolfgang alone, takes on the character of a high-class freak show.
Koblenz (**8**)	The children give one concert.
Bonn (**9**)	They pass through Beethoven's future birthplace without engagements.
Aix-la-Chapelle (**10**)	The children perform for Princess Amalia of Prussia, sister of Frederick the Great, who was taking the waters.
Brussels (**11**)	After weeks of inattention, they finally play for Prince Charles of Lorraine, and move on to Paris.
Paris (**12**)	The children give many concerts and become the darlings of the nobility. Wolfgang composes three violin sonatas.

1764

London (**13**)	The children play for George III; Wolfgang becomes friends with J.C. Bach; composes his first four symphonies; many concerts.

1765

Lille (**14**)	Illness delays the family's progress by a month.
Ghent (**15**)	Wolfgang tries a new organ.
Antwerp (**16**)	Wolfgang plays in the cathedral to great acclaim.
The Hague (**17**)	The family is graciously received by William, Prince of Orange. Wolfgang is put through his usual paces.

1766

Amsterdam (**18**)	Wolfgang's latest symphony (in B flat, K.22) is publicly performed.
The Hague (**19**)	He composes six more violin sonatas (K.26–31) and the humorous *Gallimathias musicum*, K.32.
Paris (**20**)	Numerous performances at the palace of Versailles; Wolfgang composes Kyrie in F, K.33, his first church music.
Geneva, Berne, Zürich (**21–3**)	
Donaueschingen (**24**)	The children play on nine occasions from five until nine in the evening.
Munich (**25**)	The children appear before the Elector.
Salzburg (**26**)	The family returns on 29 or 30 November after three and a half years.

When, after almost a year and a half, all the proper concert venues had been exhausted, Leopold went for free enterprise, announcing on bills and in the papers that whoever was curious could visit the family at home 'Every Day in the Week from Twelve to Two o'clock, and have an Opportunity of putting the young Mozart's Talents to a more particular Proof, by giving him any thing to play at Sight, or any Music without a Bass, which he will write upon the Spot without recurring [sic] to his Harpsichord'.

By 8 July 1765, Leopold had discovered a new venue, as evidenced by a notice in the *Public Advertiser*:

> To all Lovers of Sciences.
>
> THE greatest Prodigy that Europe, or that even Human Nature has to boast of, is, without Contradiction, the little German Boy WOLFGANG MOZART; a Boy, Eight Years old, who has, and indeed very justly, raised the Admiration not only of the greatest Men, but also of the greatest Musicians in Europe. It is hard to say, whether his Execution upon the Harpsichord and his playing and singing at Sight, or his own Caprice, Fancy, and Compositions for all Instruments, are most astonishing. The Father of this Miracle, being obliged by Desire of several Ladies and Gentlemen to postpone, for a very short Time, his Departure from England, will give an Opportunity to hear this little Composer and his Sister, whose musical Knowledge wants not Apology. Performs every Day in the Week, from Twelve to Three o'Clock in the Great Room, at the Swan and Hoop, Cornhill. Admittance 2s. 6d. each Person.
>
> The two Children will play also together with four Hands upon the same Harpsichord, and put upon it a Handkerchief, without seeing the Keys.

Mr. Mozart, who has been obliged by the Desire of several Ladies and Gentlemen to postpone his Departure from England for a short Time, takes this Opportunity to inform the Public, that he has taken the great Room in the Swan and Harp Tavern in Cornhill, where he will give an opportunity to all the Curious to hear these two young Prodigies perform every Day from Twelve to Three. Admittance 2 shillings and sixpence each person.

Newspaper cutting recognising Mozart's prodigious talent

Far more significant than the concerts and the sideshows, however, was the burgeoning friendship between Mozart and Johann Christian Bach, youngest (and in England the most famous) son of Johann Sebastian. It was in London, too, that Mozart began to compose in earnest: under the influence of J.C.

Bach he wrote his first symphonies, having now, in reality, advanced to the age of nine. J.C. Bach's musical style had a formative influence on Mozart's own, and it was probably he, more than anyone, who fired the young Mozart with his love of Italian opera (J.C. Bach's stock-in-trade for many years).

When the Mozarts finally returned to Salzburg after their three-and-a-half-year jaunt, they were probably, outside royalty, the most famous family in Europe. Thanks to Leopold's near-ruthless genius as an impresario, they were almost certainly the richest musicians as well, though Leopold took considerable pains to conceal the fact.

Leopold kept his official position at the court, but after an absence of almost four years it was clear that he was more valuable as a travelling musical ambassador than as a court musician. He, and more to the point his children, had made Salzburg a household name all over Europe. There was no one more keenly aware than Leopold that the children's marketability depended on their youth After a mere nine months, therefore, the family took to the road once more, this time bound for Vienna, where they stayed for the best part of a year.

By the time they got back to Salzburg in January 1769, Mozart, now nearly thirteen, had put behind him ten symphonies, two operas, eighteen sonatas for piano and violin, three masses, several other religious choral works, and four piano concertos . Most of the year 1769 was spent, for a change, at home in Salzburg, where he chalked up a further two masses and another couple of symphonies. It was in this year, too, that he wrote the first letter to have come down to us. It is a brief note to an unidentified girl, also in Salzburg:

Dear Friend,
Pardon me for taking the liberty of writing to you, but as you said
you could understand everything in Latin, no matter what I might

write down, curiosity has overcome me so I am sending you a few lines of various Latin words. When you have read them, please favour me with a reply. But you too must send a proper letter. So: Cuperem scire de qua causa, a quam plurimis adolescentibus otium usque adeo aestimatur, ut ipsi se nec verbis, nec verberibus, ab hoc sinant abduci. *And there you are!*

This translates as: 'I should like to know why laziness is so much prized by young men that neither by words nor blows will they suffer themselves to be roused from it!' The use of two or more languages in a single letter became almost habitual with Mozart, particularly when writing to his sister.

Nannerl was now eighteen, and no longer marketable as a child prodigy. When Leopold next set off, this time to Italy, it was with Wolfgang alone. With the boy's brief letters home during this first Italian trip, we embark on a treasure trove of autobiographical evidence that gives us perhaps the most fully rounded portrait of any composer in history. His first letter to his mother was written shortly after their departure from Salzburg and well before their arrival in Italy:

Dearest Mama,

My heart is overjoyed with the delights of this trip, because the journey is such fun, and our coachman drives tremendously fast whenever the road allows it. Papa, of course, has already told you about our journey. The reason I am writing to you now is to demonstrate that I know my duty and am, with the deepest respect, your devoted son,

Wolfgang Mozart

In Italy he fulfilled at last a wish he had nourished ever since meeting J.C. Bach in London. Like Handel before him, it had been in Italy itself that J.C. Bach had learned the craft of writing Italian opera. Far more exciting to Mozart than the two concerts he gave shortly after their arrival in Verona were his two visits to the opera house. In Milan he met the highly cultured and influential Count Firmian, who secured a commission for him to write an opera for the next winter season in that already operatic city. Father and son then moved on to Bologna and Florence, making important and influential acquaintances in each, and in April 1770 they reached Rome, armed with some twenty letters of introduction to the aristocracy and clergy. Before they could proffer even one of them, however, they found themselves, as Leopold relates, only inches away from the highest figure of all:

Mozart's letter to his mother, 13 December 1769 (translated on opposite page)

On our arrival, following lunch, we went to St Peter's, and thence to Mass. On the twelfth we were present at the Functiones, and when the Pope was serving the poor at table we came within touching distance, as we found ourselves standing beside him at the top of the table. This incident was all the more amazing as we had had to pass through two doors under the scrutiny of two armed guards and make our way through a crowd of many hundreds. Remember that we had as yet no acquaintances in the city at all. But our fine clothes and my customary authoritative manner helped us through everywhere. They seem to have mistaken Wolfgang for some German courtier, some even thought that he was a prince, and I myself was taken for his tutor. And so we made our way to the Cardinals' table. There Wolfgang himself was standing between the chairs of two Cardinals, one of whom, as luck would have it, was Cardinal Pallavicini, to whom we had, and were carrying, a letter of introduction.

Later they would meet the Pope himself, but before that the most famous incident of the entire journey occurred.

In the Sistine Chapel they heard the famous *Miserere* by the seventeenth-century composer Gregorio Allegri – famous not only for its beauty but for the fact that it was strictly forbidden to remove even a page of this much prized work from the chapel, on pain of excommunication. This troubled the young Mozart not a whit: on returning to their lodgings, he sat down and wrote out the entire work from memory.

It was also in Rome that the Pope conferred on him the rarely awarded Order of the Golden Spur, making him officially a knight – the first time the honour had ever been bestowed on a mere fourteen-year-old. Mozart, of course, was never a 'mere' fourteen-year-old, but he was only fourteen, and in many ways, despite his musical precocity and grace of manner, he remained very much a child. This disarming combination of maturity and childish innocence emerges clearly in his first correspondence. Most of these early 'letters' are no more than scribbled messages written at the end of letters from Leopold. From Naples he reports:

I too am still alive and as happy as ever, and I simply adore travelling! And to think that I have now been on the Mediterranean! Vesuvius is smoking furiously today – thunder and lightning and all the rest of it. I had a great desire today to ride on a donkey, since it's the custom in Italy, and so I thought that I too should try it.

Mixed in with these chatty asides are hints of that keen observation of character which would later help to make him the greatest operatic composer who had ever lived:

We are currently travelling with a certain Dominican, who is regarded as a holy man. Personally, I don't believe a word of it, for at breakfast he'll frequently take a cup of chocolate and then immediately follow it up with a good glass of strong Spanish wine. I myself have had the privilege of lunching with this saint, who on this occasion drank a whole decanter and finished up with a full glass of very strong wine, two big slices of melon, some peaches and pears for dessert, five cups of coffee, a whole plate of cloves and two full dishes of milk and lemon. I suppose he might be following some sort of diet, but I doubt it, for it would be too much; and anyway he eats like this at every meal and what's more, stokes himself up with several snacks during the afternoon as well.

In between the touring and the sightseeing, the socialising and the concerts, Mozart was fantastically productive, writing in the space of time between his letters more music than he could keep track of:

Several times now, I have had the pleasure of going alone to a beautiful church, and to some magnificent services there. In the meantime I've composed four Italian symphonies, not to mention arias for my opera, of which I must already have composed half a dozen at least, and even a motet!

Even as a child, Mozart never shrank from self-congratulation. Yet no composer was ever more extravagantly praised or widely admired by others from his earliest remembered years. On the face of it, there was certainly no need to blind his mother and sister with statistics. At a deeper level, however, a merely unattractive trait may have its poignant aspect in his continuing anxiety, probably subconscious, that love was something that he had to earn through performance and achievement. This was surely the message he got from his father – and never before had he and his father been thrown together so closely and for so long as on this Italian journey. Fear and hero worship, particularly when the object of each is one's father, are intimately connected. As he stood on the cusp between childhood and adolescence, Mozart naturally assumed what he took to be an adult pose by imitating the style and outlook of his father. In a postscript to one of Leopold's letters home, he wrote to his mother with exactly the same mixture of condescension and self-assured advice that Leopold dispensed on an almost daily basis:

It grieves me to hear that poor Martha has been so ill, and I hope that with God's help she will recover. If she doesn't, however, we must not be unduly distressed, for God's will is always best and He certainly knows best whether it is right for us to be in this world or in the next. She should console herself with the thought that after the rain she may enjoy the sunshine.

Thus did a fourteen-year-old boy instruct his mother in the comfort of the dying. The Martha in question was only five years older than Mozart himself and died before he and Leopold got back to Salzburg.

With the coming of the summer season, the steady diet of concerts and privately arranged performances that had been the Mozarts' daily bread diminished. Wolfgang spent the rest of 1770 largely on the composition of the opera for Milan, *Mitridate, rè di Ponto*, based on a famous tragedy by Racine. It had its premiere on the day after Christmas. Mozart himself conducted the first three performances, and from the beginning it was a roaring success.

After the auspicious launch of his first truly Italian opera (his earlier *opera buffa* – comic opera – *La finta semplice* had been for Vienna), there were no pressing reasons to stay in Italy. Leopold, however, seemed in no great hurry to go home, so they lingered for a few months more, first in Turin, then in Venice. Mozart gave many concerts, all of them sensationally received, and father and son slowly wended their way back to Salzburg. They arrived there, after an absence of fifteen months, at the end of March 1771. In their luggage was a contract for a second opera in Milan, *Lucio Silla*; shortly after their return came another commission, for a third opera, *Ascanio in Alba*, this one also for Milan. And so it was, a mere five months after their return home, that Mozart and his father embarked upon their second Italian adventure.

Ascanio in Alba was to form only part of the lavish festivities leading up to the marriage of the Archduke Ferdinand and Princess Maria Beatrice Ricciarda. These were also to include a raft of other theatrical productions, musical and dramatic, horse races, masked balls, a series of opulent banquets at the court, and a special mass wedding at which 150 young couples would be publicly united and presented with dowries by the royal pair themselves. The entire city was to be brilliantly illuminated, fountains would flow with wine instead of water, and *Ascanio* was to be the crowning glory of the celebrations. When the great day came, it scored such a resounding success that it was repeated, by public demand, two days later. At fifteen, Mozart the composer of Italian opera had arrived.

Journey 2: 1769–71

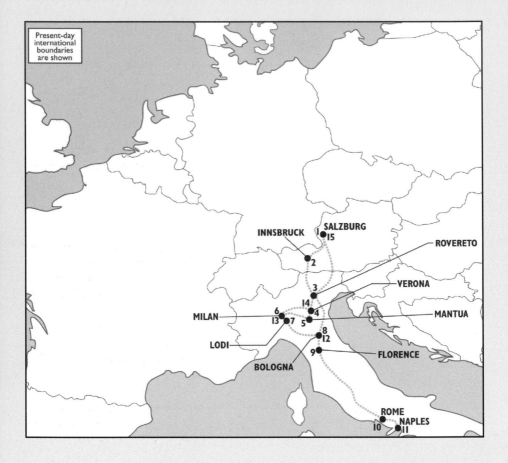

Origin: Salzburg (1)

1769

Innsbruck (2)   Mozart is graciously received by Count Spaur; he gives a concert with a violinist, a horn player and an organist.

Rovereto (Italy) (3)   Mobbed by admirers and the curious, he is scarcely able to reach the organ for his concert at the principal church.

Verona (4)   The same, but still more so; journalists, poets and painters vie with each other to extol and portray the boy wonder.

1770

Mantua (5)   Mozart attracts similar attentions, this time mostly from women; two of his symphonies are performed, interspersed with 'freak show' tricks and tests.

Milan (6)   Concert at the palace of Count Firmian leads to Mozart's first operatic commission, for the following Christmas.

Lodi (7)   Mozart composes his first string quartet.

Bologna (8)   Meets and is befriended by the great theorist and teacher Padre Giovanni Battista Martini (64) and the great castrato singer Farinelli.

Florence (9)   Plays with the famous violinist-composer Pietro Nardini; composes several canons and the Kyrie, K.89; befriends the English prodigy Thomas Linley.

Rome (10)   Hears Allegri's *Miserere* and later writes it out from memory; receives from the Pope the Order of the Golden Spur.

Naples (11)   Meets the eminent composer Niccolò Jommelli (56) and the travelling English musician and historian Dr Charles Burney.

Bologna (12)   Has lessons from Padre Martini and is elected a member of the Philharmonic Society after writing an elaborate contrapuntal test piece.

Milan (13)   Completes his opera *Mitridate, rè di Ponto* and sees it produced with great success; writes four more symphonies (K.74, 84, 95, 97).

1771

Verona (14)   Receives the title of *Maestro di cappella* from the Accademia Filarmonica.

Salzburg (15)   Mozart and his father return via Padua, Vicenza and Verona. Mozart has a new operatic commission for Milan.

Interlude II: The Music of the Child

Before even reaching his teens, Mozart had composed works in virtually every genre that was to distinguish his adult output: numerous solo piano pieces, some of the first (possibly *the* first) music ever composed for piano duet (two players at one keyboard), chamber music (eighteen sonatas for piano and violin, minuets for mixed instruments), two operas, choral music (including two masses and other works for four-part choir, orchestra and organ), at least ten symphonies, four piano concertos (arranged from other men's music), and songs for voice and piano.

We can never know, of course, just how much of Leopold there is in the earliest works – composed between 1761, when Wolfgang was five, and 1768 – but there is no reason to doubt their overall authenticity. No father in Leopold's situation could be expected to withhold all comments and suggestions from a child of that age, and in any case, as we have seen, Leopold was his children's only teacher – and not just in music. His influence was all-pervasive. As the earliest pieces for keyboard are written in Leopold's hand, it can be assumed that Mozart composed them in his head but had not yet mastered the technique of writing them down. Nor are the pieces themselves anything like works of genius. Apart from the fact that they were composed by a five-year-old, there is nothing particularly remarkable in any of them.

We know them today – and children are given them to play – only because of what Mozart did later. On purely musical grounds they would long since have sunk without trace.

When we turn from these very early piano pieces to Mozart's First Symphony, composed when he was eight, we seem to enter another world. The reasons, however, have less to do with genius *Mozart's father* than with the natural changes of any normal child between the *Leopold*

ages of five and eight. Apart from the question of length, the use of an orchestra adds immeasurably to the impressiveness of the music. Then there is the filling out of the harmony: the use of successive chords instead of the simple, two-part melody-and-accompaniment texture of those first minuets. This is, indeed, a genuine and significant advance. But one would expect no less, at eight, of a child who could turn out keyboard minuets at five.

For a balanced assessment of these first symphonies, a certain amount of demystification is in order. Melodies consist of scale fragments and/or spelt-out chords. Harmony results from the simultaneous sounding of two or more notes. Both scales and spelt-out chords imply or unambiguously specify certain harmonies. At the most basic level, one might say that the scale is analogous to the alphabet, while chords are analogous to words. To generalise further, one could liken melody to nouns and verbs, and harmony to adjectives (though it also has important verb-like properties). Since most of the melodies we hear have a harmonic component, either implicit or explicit, it would be dangerous to take these analogies too literally. In the relationship of chords/harmonies, however, we do have something very like grammar in verbal language.

Any well-trained musician, of any age, will inevitably have acquired a basic vocabulary of chordal/harmonic relationships. This does not require any verbal explanation. Like verbal language it can be 'picked up' by exposure. We all speak 'prose', after all, long before we learn anything about 'parts of speech'. A remarkable number of hymn and folk tunes can be harmonised with two or three basic chords. Like clichés and idioms in verbal language, certain combinations of chords/harmonies crop up in every era like the common change of daily speech. Some of these are intrinsically expressive, like the formulaic use of 'suspensions' (see Glossary) at the opening of Mozart's First Symphony. The musical means of constructing a whole movement are an expansion of the same basic principles that govern the making of a simple minuet.

There are certain stock devices that may be used to achieve this expansion. The simplest is straight repetition, often expressively enhanced by the 'echo' effect: first time loud, second time soft. The repeated material may be anything from a scrap of melody to whole phrases. Another is the use of 'sequence', in which a single melodic figure is repeated, consecutively, at different pitches – as in the 'Gloria' of the Christmas carol *Ding, Dong Merrily on High*. Vivaldi regularly uses both devices to a dangerous degree. Mozart does likewise in his Symphony No. 1 and other early symphonies.

Indeed the structure of a whole movement in 'sonata form' – the pre-eminent design of the Classical era – is likewise a formula. Put at its crudest, it might almost be likened to 'painting by numbers'. The ground plan is very clearly laid out, the 'rules' are easy enough to follow; and for anyone properly trained in the nuts and bolts of composition, writing a 'correct' sonata movement is no great trick. Exciting and holding the listener's interest, however, is another matter. Here, the 'requirements' of the form offer very little help, being heavily reliant on repetition and memory. One of the biggest challenges to the composer of movements in sonata form is to achieve repetition without repetitiousness – that is to say, without the music becoming either boringly predictable or tedious, its charms worn thin by over-exposure. As these early symphonies reveal, mastery of this trick was not something that even Mozart acquired overnight. Among the many fascinating aspects of his first half-dozen symphonies is the opportunity they give us to eavesdrop, as it were, on the development of a great symphonist from a very early age.

Like many composers, Mozart was a natural magpie. He learned as much from observation and imitation as from instruction. What he liked, what he felt would be of use to him, he adopted. In the case of his first four keyboard concertos, on the other hand, he adapted. Written when he was eleven, they were clearly intended for his own performance. With the exception of a single movement (the *Andante* of No. 1, K.37), which may possibly be by Mozart himself, they consist entirely of arrangements. Basing them mainly on sonata movements by Raupach, Honauer, Eckard, Schobert and C.P.E. Bach, Mozart elegantly adapts the solo writing to his taste and provides orchestral introductions and accompaniments as well as writing his own cadenzas. Though hardly masterpieces, these are unfailingly attractive works. Both in their orchestration (where Mozart shows the same flair for blending strings, wind and horns already evident in his earliest symphonies) and in the interplay between soloist and orchestra, they leave no room for surprise that the piano concerto as a medium was to mark the pinnacle of Mozart's instrumental achievement.

Given that most of his concertos are strongly influenced by opera, it seems appropriate that Mozart's first explorations of the genre should coincide with his debut as a theatrical composer. It is interesting, too, that while the concertos are fashionably contemporary, both the German 'sacred play with music' *Die Schuldigkeit des ersten Gebots* ('The Obligation to Keep the First Commandment', K.35) and the Latin comedy *Apollo et Hyacinthus* (K.38) are old-fashioned, wooden and rather dull. It is with the German operetta *Bastien und Bastienne*, from 1768, that we get our first real glimpse of the dramatist-to-be. Still the best-known of his childhood operas, it had its auspicious premiere in the garden of Dr Anton Mesmer (he of 'mesmerism' fame). This is an enchanting work, from beginning to end, with all the delightful innocence one might expect from an eighteenth-century twelve-year-old. With only one (short) act, a cast of three, a single set, and simple songs rather than proper arias, it could easily be produced at many a secondary school:

child*like*, certainly; child*ish*, no. The music is perfectly suited to the subject matter, and Mozart's gift for characterisation is already evident. In comparison, his second opera of that year, *La finta semplice* ('The Pretend Simpleton', K.51), is rather a comedown.

Before the year was out, he had also completed the series of eighteen sonatas for keyboard with violin accompaniment begun in 1762, added two masses (one lost) and an offertory, *Veni Sancte Spiritus* (K.47), to his church music, and clocked up two more symphonies (K.45 and 48). Most of the next year (1769) was spent in Salzburg, where he composed two contrasting masses: the short *Missa brevis* in D minor, K.65, and the grandly scaled 'Dominicus' Mass in C, K.66, scored for four soloists, chorus, orchestra and organ. Written to mark the first mass celebrated by Mozart's childhood friend Cajetan Hagenauer (Father Dominicus) at St Peter's Abbey in October 1769, the 'Dominicus' Mass was revived in 1774, when Leopold directed its performance at the Jesuit church 'Am Hof' in Vienna. It remains the best known of all Mozart's juvenile mass settings.

Mozart's symphonies of this period have been the subject of much speculation. He may have composed five symphonies on his first Italian journey, although the authenticity of four of these (K.81, 84, 95 and 97) has been challenged by scholars. The one irrefutably genuine symphony is K.74 in G major, which Mozart may have originally conceived as an opera overture. Dating from the same period, and composed en route from Milan to Parma, is Mozart's first string quartet, K.80. Exceeding all these works in its significance for Mozart's career, however, was the opera *Mitridate, rè di Ponto* ('Mithridates, King of Pontus'), K.87. This scored a huge success at its premiere on 26 December 1770 and was repeated twenty times in Milan alone. His first full-length opera (three acts and twenty-five numbers), it leaves the simple charms of *Bastien und Bastienne* far behind.

Based on the tragedy by Jean Racine (1639–1699), *Mitridate* represents a huge advance in ambition, if not always in achievement. Whatever his musical gifts and social sophistication, a fourteen-year-old boy can hardly be expected to probe the depths of a drama by one of the greatest tragedians in history. Admittedly, the text he was given was not original Racine but a poor adaptation by a mediocre poet (one Vittorio Amedeo Cigna-Santi). Nor had he ever attempted anything on this scale before. To sustain a drama over a stretch of some three hours is a challenge even to veterans, let alone to a young teenager. If *Mitridate* must ultimately be regarded as a failure, it is nevertheless a noble one, far surpassing in purely musical terms the work of many respectable Italian opera composers of the time. Mozart's flare for adopting the Italian style is truly virtuosic, as is his treatment of the Italian language; but the depth and vividness of characterisation needed to bring a drama such as this to life as yet lay beyond his capacities. How, indeed, could it not?

If *Ascanio in Alba*, composed less than a year later, can be considered a greater artistic success, the explanation lies not only with an advance in Mozart's capacities but with a reduction of the challenge posed. Far from being a tragedy, the text hardly amounts even to a drama, and characterisation plays a negligible role in the proceedings. It is not so much an opera as an allegorical entertainment designed to celebrate a royal marriage and divert the populace – a musical equivalent of fireworks. While *Ascanio in Alba* lacks variety and dramatic tension, it does achieve new heights of virtuosity and compositional mastery. Indeed, it can be seen as the culmination of Mozart's musical childhood.

Chapter 3

The Eternal Child

The Eternal Child

The image of Mozart as an 'eternal child' has been a long time dying. To this day, there are very many people who believe it. Throughout the nineteenth century it was the standard view. It receded considerably in the first half of the twentieth, and then received a huge boost, first through a popular biography by Wolfgang Hildesheimer, but chiefly through the play, then the film, *Amadeus*, which was heavily influenced by Hildesheimer. In contrast to the nineteenth-century image, Mozart was here presented not only as an eternal child, but as a giggling fool who, except where music was concerned, couldn't think his way out of a paper bag. Yet Mozart's genius was not only musical. Among the prime elements of his greatness as an opera composer was a remarkable insight into the complexities of human character. His unerring sense of what might be described as 'dramatic psychology' made him a theatrical as well as a musical genius. He would have made a great film director. His characters are precisely that: characters, not caricatures. Like characters in real life, they are not static. They develop – not, in most cases, because of the words they sing, but because of the music behind the words. One of the most virtuosic achievements in operatic history is the great Sextet in Act III of *The Marriage of Figaro*, where Mozart not only has six characters singing six different things at the same time but keeps them in character throughout.

As a dramatist he bears comparison with Shakespeare. From where, then, does the stereotyped image arise? Why the myth of the eternal child?

In fairness to the authors who have purveyed it, the myth derives largely from the man himself, as revealed in many of the hundreds of letters which he wrote to his family and others from the age of thirteen. The letters in question reveal a sense of humour which is not only childish but sometimes positively infantile. Before the advent of Sigmund Freud in the late nineteenth century, the idea that we retain the child in us throughout our lives was by no means universally acknowledged. In common with many creative geniuses, Mozart not only recognised this in himself but took no pains to conceal it, at least not from his family or close friends. In some respects he seems to have been entirely without inhibitions.

In one particular respect, however, he was very inhibited indeed; and the greatest drama of his life involved coming to terms with that fact. He was deeply, tragically inhibited by his father. Remember that childhood motto: 'After God, Papa'. It is with 'Papa', at least as much as with his son, that the myth of the eternal child has its source. The child Mozart had brought Leopold a degree of fame, wealth and parental power beyond his previous imaginings. His role as shepherd to 'God's miracle' came to define his sense of self. He had an ever-deepening need to be needed, and the calendar was against him. The myth became his lifeline. It was an image he fostered with dreadful care, and for a long time Mozart obliged him. Who would guess from this letter to Nannerl, five years his senior, that the author was not only a genius but already an internationally famous composer?

MILAN, 18 December 1772. I hope this finds you flourishing, my dear sister. When you get this letter, my dear sister, that very evening my opera will have been staged, my dear sister. Think hard of me, my dear sister, and try your utmost to imagine that you, my dear sister, are witnessing it too, my dear sister. That is not easy, I grant you, since it's eleven o'clock already. Otherwise I believe, indubitably, my dear sister, that during the day it is brighter than at Easter. Tomorrow we go to lunch, my dear sister, with Herr von Mayr, and why, do you suppose? Well guess! Why, because he has asked us! Which reminds me. Have you had news yet of what's just happened here? We left Count Firmian's today to go home and when we reached our street... we opened our front door... and what do you think? Why, we went in. Farewell, my little lung. I kiss you my liver, and remain as ever, my stomach, your unworthy... Oh please, please, my dear sister! Something is biting me. Do come and scratch me!

Mozart's sister Maria Anna ('Nannerl')

In the actual letter, every other line is written upside down.

Not long afterwards, at the end of their third and last visit to Italy, Mozart and his father returned to Salzburg, where Leopold immediately embarked on the next stage in his campaign to secure a prestigious position for Wolfgang. This time he had his eye on Vienna, and as usual there was a hidden agenda. It was never his plan that Mozart alone should find a position. He envisaged an arrangement in which he too would be honoured with a post at the same establishment. With his son as the chief breadwinner, the whole family would continue to thrive as a closely knit unit, with Leopold, by divine right, at its head. Since their return from Italy, the plan had taken on a new and unexpected urgency. The Prince-Archbishop Schrattenbach, who had so generously supported the Mozarts during their long Grand Tour and subsequently, had died. Succeeding him was the highly controversial Hieronymus Colloredo, who had been elected to the position only on the forty-ninth ballot. His attitude to the Mozarts was very different. He had no desire for a Vice-Kapellmeister who spent more time away from his post than at it. The Mozarts had already done their job as roving ambassadors of the Salzburg court, in the process enhancing the prestige of the resident Prince-Archbishop. Now, Colloredo reasoned, it was time for Salzburg to reap the rewards. To his credit, he kept Mozart well supplied with commissions, which produced many fine works. In the final nine months of 1773 alone Mozart produced, among other things, seven symphonies, six string quartets, a string quintet, four divertimentos, sixteen orchestral dances, a mass, and his first entirely original piano concerto, K.175 in D, which he kept in his repertoire for years afterwards.

In 1773 Salzburg could hardly be described as a musical backwater, but it was a distinct come-down from the main cultural centres of Europe in which Mozart had spent most of his professional life. With his steadily worsening relationship with Colloredo, Mozart was now as eager as his father to find an official position appropriate to his genius and proven accomplishment. Indeed, leaving Salzburg became his principal worldly ambition. It was thus in high hopes that Leopold and Wolfgang set off in July for Vienna, the capital city not only of Austria but of the ancient (and by now distinctly unholy) Holy Roman Empire. Leopold, confident that he had devised a winning strategy, adopted an air of cloak-and-dagger secrecy that would not have been out of place in one of his son's operas:

There are many things about which it is best not to write. And at all costs we must avoid anything which might cause a stir or trigger suspicion either here or, especially, at Salzburg, or which might give our enemies a chance to put a spoke in our wheel.

As it turned out, father and son returned to Salzburg with nothing to show, Leopold embittered and Wolfgang seething with a mixture of disappointment and resentment which may account for the darkness that shadows some of the music he wrote on their return. By general consent, Symphony No. 25 in G minor, K.183 was his first indisputable masterpiece, the work in which his own individual voice as a composer emerges crystal clear for the first time.

Back in Salzburg once again, Mozart put his Viennese disappointment behind him and immersed himself in composition. Writing, whether musical compositions or letters, was a great therapy for Mozart. Accordingly, he kept himself busy. He had no time for the self-pity which would all but engulf his father in years to come. He was naturally resilient, and he knew better than anyone that his genius was now in full flower. Most of the music he composed from this time onwards was unmistakably his own, no longer imitative of older, more experienced composers.

For most of 1774 Mozart was homebound but far from idle. The tally for that year included three more symphonies, two concertos, two masses, several other sacred works, a serenade, and a full-length opera, *La finta giardiniera*, composed for Munich. That occupied him for the last four months of the year, and it was only in late December, when he travelled to Munich to prepare for its performance, that he started writing letters again. One letter in particular was immediately seized on by early biographers, as it is the first time that Mozart specifically mentions a girl in a romantic or sexual context. As he wrote to his sister:

Please give my best wishes to Roxelana, and ask her to have tea this afternoon with the Sultan. And please give every kind of message to Mademoiselle Mitzerl, and assure her of my undying love. Visions of her, clad only in her négligée, are ever before my eyes. I must admit that attractive girls abound here, and in faith I have seen many, but none, none so ravishing as she is.

'Mademoiselle Mitzerl' was in fact the sixty-four-year-old grandmother who had recently become the Mozarts' new landlady in Salzburg. Wolfgang's high spirits had obviously returned.

For all the masterly music that seemed to pour out of him, Mozart was biding his time. He longed to escape from Salzburg into the bigger world where he belonged; but whether or not he was yet able to admit it to himself, he also longed to get away from his father. He may have been a musical genius but he was also a late teenager, who needed, like most late teenagers, to spread his wings. Here was a boy who had been in the close company of his father for practically every waking hour of his life. Never having been to school, and having lived a predominantly peripatetic life, he had had relatively little contact with other children of his age. Among the few significant exceptions to this was his brief friendship with the young English violinist Thomas Linley – a musical prodigy himself, and Mozart's exact contemporary – whom he met during a short visit to Florence in 1770, when they were both fourteen. When they parted, tears were shed by both, but they were never to meet again. Eight years later, Linley died from drowning at the age of twenty-two. As with many other prodigies, Mozart's childhood had been largely stolen from him.

For as long as either of the Mozart children could remember, and what probably seemed like forever to their mother, Leopold had ruled the roost unchallenged. The others tiptoed around him, fearful of offending him, still more fearful of the likely consequences. Like many domineering fathers, 'Papa' Mozart was extraordinarily un-self-aware. The time was not far off when he would so badly miscalculate the effect of his own words that he would force the separation of himself and his son.

In 1777 the now twenty-one-year-old Mozart composed a work whose greatness and originality eclipsed everything he had written to date. It was a piano concerto. Ironically, it was written not for himself but for a French pianist who happened to be passing through Salzburg. To this day we know no more about her than her name – Mlle Jeunehomme – and not even her full name. How much she had to do with Mozart's inspiration we can never know, but she must have been an exceptional pianist. Where did she come from? Where did she go? Why is there no other trace of her existence? Is she the same as the Madame Jenomé in Paris mentioned (once each) in letters from Wolfgang and Leopold?

Whoever she was, this great concerto (K.271 in E flat) marked Mozart's coming-of-age as an artist. And he knew it. Never yet had he been in a stronger position to find employment elsewhere. He had distinguished himself in virtually every branch of musical art, and was widely regarded as the greatest living keyboard player. He was also a skilled and experienced violinist and conductor. Knowing his time had arrived, he took a decision befitting his coming-of-age: he decided to resign his post. Once again a letter was ghost-written by his father:

Your Princely Grace, Most Worthy Prince of the Holy Roman Empire, Most Gracious Ruler and Lord! Parents make the most strenuous efforts to enable their children to venture out into the world and become their own breadwinners; this they owe both to themselves and to the greater good of the state. And the more they are blessed with talent by God, the more it is their duty to make use of it and improve their own as well as their parents' lives, to help

their parents and take their progress and future in hand. The
Gospel teaches us to take advantage of our talent in this way.

The letter continues like this to the inevitable conclusion.
Leopold had overplayed his hand. The Archbishop did not need
theological instruction from a twenty-one-year-old servant. In
any case, he would have spotted at once that the style and
character of the petition came straight from Leopold. Wolfgang's
only contribution to the document had been his dutiful signature
at the bottom. As a psychological mastermind, it would seem that
Leopold was losing his grip. The Archbishop's terse response to
the letter was to fire both of them:

Father and son are granted permission to seek their fortune
elsewhere – according to the Gospel.

It was a catastrophe. For the first time in his life Leopold was out
of a job, and Wolfgang had been ignominiously sacked rather
than graciously released. The only hope was for Leopold to throw
himself on the Archbishop's mercy and plead for reinstatement,
on the clear understanding that he would not be allowed to leave
Salzburg for any reason. He was duly reinstated. Wolfgang on the
other hand was free to go and do whatever he liked. What he
would have liked was to strike out on his own, at last; but it was
not to be. Leopold was not a man easily thwarted. If he could not
be on hand to direct the show, he would do it by remote control.

As Maynard Solomon has observed, the traditional roles of
parent and child were in certain crucial ways reversed in
Wolfgang's childhood and early youth. The phenomenon,
however, was by no means confined to the Mozarts. Many an
exploited prodigy, in whatever field, can tell a similar story. The
'stage mother', a familiar monster on the early twentieth-century
entertainment scene, has been largely superseded by the

'Hollywood mother'; but the breed lives on. In Mozart's case it was the 'stage father', who unlike most of his modern counterparts was himself a man of distinction with a genius on his hands. Fired by a messianic zeal, he saw himself, remember, as a 'good, upright citizen' whose 'humble obligation' was 'to proclaim to the world a miracle, ordained by God, in the town of Salzburg'. Echoes of the Christ child have reverberated ever since. There are those who believe to this day that Mozart's birth was nothing less than the Second Coming, confirmed by his premature death at a comparable age. Leopold, however, was not a reincarnation of the Virgin Mary. His miracle was not only a child but a highly profitable commodity.

Well before his tenth birthday, Wolfgang was the family's principal breadwinner. It was the child who won fame and fortune for the family, and especially for the father. It was the child who brought comfort and security to the parents, who opened up unimagined opportunities and an entrée into the society of kings, queens and emperors. Leopold could never get over his family's unofficial elevation to the aristocracy. As he haughtily remarked in a letter to his friend Lorenz Hagenauer in Salzburg, 'We do not associate with anyone but the nobility and other distinguished personages, and receive from them nothing but the most exceptional courtesies and respect.' He also allowed himself to be flatteringly misrepresented as 'Kapellmeister' at the Salzburg court.

When the emerging man outgrew the child and the shepherd lost his sheep, however, Leopold was deprived of what had come to be his *raison d'être*. It was he, not his son, who was the dependent. As Maynard Solomon observes, the real eternal child of the Mozart family was not Wolfgang but Leopold. Another feature of the real (as opposed to the mythical) child common to all exploited prodigies was the power that Mozart could wield over audiences and family alike. There is no sign that he abused this, but one cannot read the letters of his family and others without gaining the impression that he was both conscious of and pleased by it. On being coolly rebuffed by Madame de Pompadour, mistress of Louis XV, he allegedly remarked: 'Who is this that refuses to kiss me? The Empress kissed me.' If true, this is a welcome corrective to the unblemished picture of the child Mozart as an angel straight from heaven.

The concept of the eternal child, though often used pejoratively ('the genius who never grew up') is not an ignoble one. Eternal childhood does not preclude maturity. It can not only co-exist with maturity but also enrich it. We lose the child in us to our peril. We also, however, romanticise childhood as a concept. Mozart's uninhibited playfulness, the infantile 'naughtiness' of his humour in adulthood, is innocent enough. At worst it is embarrassing. But he brought into adulthood, as he had perhaps suppressed in his years as a prodigy, an aspect of childhood which is far from innocent. There was in his make-up a lack of charity. He was by his own admission a petty bully. In the last year of his life he wrote to his wife Constanze:

I gave [Leutgeb] a surprise today. First of all I went to the Rehbergs. Well, Frau Rehberg sent one of her daughters upstairs to tell him that a dear old friend had come from Rome and had searched all the houses in the town without being able to find him. He sent down a message to say would I please wait for a few minutes. Meanwhile the poor fellow put on his Sunday best, his finest clothes, and turned up with his hair most elaborately dressed. You can imagine how we made fun of him. You know I can never resist making a fool of someone.

Joseph Leutgeb was no fool. (Mozart did not mess around with fools.) He was a good violinist and a superb horn player (all Mozart's horn concertos and the Quintet in E flat, K.407/386c were written for him) who had moved from Salzburg to Vienna, where he became a prosperous cheese merchant. Twelve years Mozart's senior, he became a good friend and a frequent victim of Mozart's least exalted humour. According to Otto Jahn, Mozart's foremost nineteenth-century biographer, Mozart would throw all the parts of his concertos and symphonies about the room and cajole Leutgeb into collecting every one of them on all fours and putting them in order. On another occasion Leutgeb was forced to kneel down behind the stove while Mozart composed. The manuscript of the Second Horn Concerto bears the inscription: 'Wolfgang Amadeus Mozart takes pity on Leutgeb, ass, ox, and simpleton, at Vienna, 27 March 1783.' It would seem, after all, that the eternal child was not Leopold's invention.

Interlude III: The Keyboard Music

With Mozart, keyboard basically means the fortepiano. Although he famously dubbed the organ 'the king of instruments', he wrote very little for it, and nothing unaccompanied. The late masterpieces which are nowadays played on the conventional organ (the Fantasia in F minor, K.608, and the *Andante* in Γ major, K.616) were actually written for a mechanical organ, though he later arranged them for piano duet. Interestingly, the quality of his nineteen piano sonatas is nothing like as consistent as the quality of his piano concertos; and they play a far less significant role in his musical life than the piano sonatas of Haydn and Beethoven do in theirs (Haydn's sixty-two are far more adventurous and wide-ranging, and Beethoven's thirty-two, taken as a whole, are the most important ever written). This is not to say that Mozart's are negligible. Some of them are indeed great works.

Mozart was an eminently practical composer. For the most part, he wrote music to order, be it an external commission, a requirement of his salaried position or the demands of his life as a freelance. Where the solo keyboard music is concerned, virtually all of it was composed for his own use. At the same time, he had learned from his father to keep a keen eye on the musical market-place. This may explain why his solo piano works (written, after all, by one of the greatest keyboard virtuosos in history) are, with few exceptions, well within the technical grasp of the moderately accomplished amateur. In a still acutely stratified society, the keyboard (harpsichord or fortepiano) was the instrument *par excellence* of the middle-class drawing-room. Accordingly, works written for it – including those involving other instruments – were regarded by many of the upper class as intrinsically inferior to quartets and quintets for strings. These, by contrast, were among the pleasures of the aristocrat and connoisseur, the province of professional musicians and the most gifted amateurs. It was a part of Mozart's genius that he succeeded in pleasing both camps at once, though few in his lifetime probably knew more than a handful of his sonatas.

Unlike Beethoven and Liszt, Mozart was not a composer who forced the keyboard's evolution by regularly writing beyond its capabilities. Like Chopin after him, he was a keen follower of fashion (indeed, his near-mania for the finest clothing was a significant factor in his financial difficulties). His interest in every advance of the piano's design and mechanism, however, had nothing to do with fashion. As a musician he was incorruptible. His knowledge of the piano was a match for that of its foremost builders and designers, and every advance in its development was reflected in the music he wrote for it. His letters on the subject reveal not only his expertise but much about his aesthetic outlook and stylistic priorities. Indeed his correspondence reveals more, perhaps, about his ideals of practical performance than that of any other composer. In a famous letter to his father, he writes:

I shall begin at once with Stein's fortepianos. Before I had seen any of his make, Späth's claviers were my favourites. But now I much prefer Stein's, for they damp very much better than the Regensburg instruments. When I strike hard, I can keep my finger on the note or raise it, but the sound ceases the moment I have

produced it. In whatever way I touch the keys, the tone is always
even. It never jars, it is never stronger or weaker or entirely
absent; in a word, it is always even. It is true that he does not sell
a pianoforte of this kind for less than three hundred gulden, but
the trouble and the labour that Stein puts into the making of it
cannot be paid for. His instruments have this splendid advantage
over others, that they are made with an escape action. Only one
maker in a hundred bothers about this. But without an
escapement it is impossible to avoid jangling and vibration after
the note is struck. When you touch the keys, the hammers fall
back again the moment after they have struck the strings, whether
you hold down the keys or release them.

Ironically and significantly, Mozart's most immediately
engaging piano sonatas are arguably not the solo sonatas but
the works for piano duet (four hands at one keyboard) and the
Sonata in D for two pianos, K.448. Ironically, because Mozart
himself was the greatest pianist of his time, and significantly,
because it supports the claim that he was essentially an opera
composer. Evidence abounds in his music that the essence of
his genius lay in characterisation and dialogue: not in an
'intellectual', Platonic exchange of philosophical positions, but
in the continuous interaction of two or more clearly
differentiated characters. If extra-musical proof were needed, in
his Sonata Movement in B flat, K.372a for solo piano, he actually
writes the name 'Sophie' (a reference to his sister-in-law) over
the opening 'sigh' of bar 71, and the name 'Constanze' (his wife)
over the more darkly harmonised answering sigh of bar 72. But
how much better it is, for true dialogue, to have two pianists at
the same keyboard – or, better still, at two different (and
spatially differentiated) pianos! Here, surely, lies the explanation
for the superiority of the duo sonatas over most of the solo ones.
Also masterpieces are the sunny *Andante and Variations* for

piano duet, K.501 and the powerful, even tragic *Adagio and Fugue* in C minor, K.426, for two pianos.

As suggested above, Mozart's greatest music is intrinsically dramatic. Almost equally intrinsic are the absence of melodrama and the relative scarcity of 'theatrical' incident. The nature of the drama in Mozart (indeed in most music) is almost entirely psychological. For this reason, it should come as no surprise to find it perfectly described in a book which has nothing to do with music. In *Aspects of the Novel*, the great English writer E.M. Forster unknowingly delivers one of the best and most fundamental music lessons ever given, for listeners, performers and composers alike:

> *Let us define a plot. We have defined a story as a narrative of events arranged in their time-sequence. A plot is also a narrative of events, the emphasis falling on causality. 'The king died and then the queen died' is a story. 'The king died, and then the queen died of grief' is a plot. The time-sequence is preserved, but the sense of causality overshadows it. Or again: 'The queen died, no one knew why, until it was discovered that it was through grief at the death of the king.' This is a plot with a mystery in it, a form capable of high development. It suspends the time-sequence, it moves as far away from the story as its limitations will allow. Consider the death of the queen. If it is in a story we say 'and then?' If it is in a plot we ask 'why?' That is the fundamental difference between these two aspects of the novel.*

It is also the fundamental difference between a great and a merely good composer. In great music, the queen always dies for a reason.

The operatic element in Mozart's music exists primarily in three dimensions. One, perfectly articulated in Forster's definition of a plot, is the element of dialogue: the continuous chain of cause and effect, statement and response (Constanze: Sophie). Another is the lyric nature of his invention: melody abounds; his music always sings. And the third, without which the other two could never work as they do, is his gift for characterisation. Mozart's themes are rarely neutral. He was a portraitist in sound. The slow movement of his Piano Sonata in C, K.309 is a particularly specific case in point: 'I wanted here,' he wrote, 'to compose an andante in accordance with Mlle Rose's character. And it is quite true to say that as Mlle Cannabich is, so is the andante.' These three dimensions are essential to any first-rate performance of a Mozart work, but they can also greatly enhance the enjoyment and appreciation of the listener who is aware of them. Mozart's highly developed gift for characterisation is also one of the main reasons why his writing for woodwind remains in a class of its own. Unlike the piano or a string ensemble of any size, each woodwind instrument has a very particular character of sound, which plays into the hands of a master psychologist like Mozart. The pianist, unfortunately, has no such luxury. The overall similarity of tone in the middle register of the piano, where most of Mozart's piano writing is set, makes vivid characterisation an especially difficult and subtle challenge. Over-characterisation − caricature − is an almost greater danger than under-characterisation. Mozart was the mortal enemy of exaggeration in all its forms. Add to this the extraordinarily simple, translucent nature of Mozart's piano textures, which give the player no place to hide (rarely does Mozart even have a solid chord in the left hand), and Artur Schnabel's famous remark makes perfect sense: 'Mozart's piano sonatas are too easy for beginners and too difficult for artists.' A great performance of a Mozart sonata is a major achievement.

If the piano sonatas are undercover operas, several of them are also undercover concertos, none more so than the B flat Sonata, K.333, whose Rondo finale has a written-out cadenza, after which the 'orchestra' returns to round off the movement. A similar instance is the finale of the earlier B flat Sonata, K.281. Less obvious is the fact that, while Mozart always writes idiomatically for the piano, he seems often to be thinking of it as a kind of surrogate orchestra. Even in the comparatively early Sonata in D, K.284, there is an orchestral spaciousness, pomp and grandeur. This is both the best and most difficult of the early sonatas, definitely not average amateur fare. Mozart himself was particularly fond of it and continued to perform it throughout his career.

The most popular of the sonatas has long been the A major, K.331. Unusually, this contains no movement in sonata form: it opens with a Theme and Variations, continues with a Menuet and ends with the famous 'Turkish March' Rondo (another highly 'orchestral' piece). The 'easy' Sonata in C, K.545 is also well known, partly through having been given to so many hapless pupils, who have discovered the hard way that it is not easy at all. Apart from these two sonatas, none could really be described as popular. The greatest, in the view of many musicians and music lovers, is the dark and turbulent Sonata in A minor, K.310, composed in the immediate aftermath of his mother's death and, at its time, the most anguished and violent sonata ever written.

Also dark and tragic are the great Sonata in C minor, K.457 and its numerical anagram, the wild and unpredictable Fantasia in C minor, K.475, which was originally designed to precede it (the two are often played in tandem). Many musicians have equal time for the last of all, the overtly contrapuntal Sonata in D, K.576 and for the big Sonata in F, K.533, likewise contrapuntally inclined and incorporating, as its finale, the separately numbered Rondo in F, K.494.

Remarkable, too, are a number of free-standing works. These include the highly chromatic, almost unbearably lonely *Adagio* in B minor, K.540; the even more chromatic Minuet in D, K.355

Manuscript extract of Mozart's Sonata in A minor, K.310, signed at the top (possibly the last piano piece he ever wrote, despite its relatively early numbering); and the poignant, melancholic (and, again, intensely chromatic) Rondo in A minor, K.511, which bears a strong resemblance to Chopin's famous waltz in the same key. Of Mozart's sixteen self-contained sets of variations, only two, K.455 and 460, come close to being major works. All, though, are attractive, several ingenious, and some, like the Variations on *Ah, vous dirai-je, Maman*, K.265 (better known to English speakers as 'Twinkle, Twinkle, Little Star'), are amusing as well as clever.

Chapter 4

Mozart Marooned

Mozart Marooned

In 1777 Mozart had legally come of age, and was his own man. Leopold, predictably, was having none of it – and with some justification. Pampered and cared for all his life, Mozart, in many practical respects, remained a babe in arms. It was all part of Leopold's script. Where, after all, would Mozart be without his old father to pack for him and look after his clothes and take care of appointments and a hundred other little things? Suppose he were to catch a bad cold without 'Papa' there to take care of him? No, my poor dear boy. If Papa cannot accompany you, then your beloved Mama will have to go in his stead. In truth, Leopold was deeply fearful of his son's independence, and more frightened still by the prospect of his being ensnared by women, duped into marriage and fathering a family of his own.

'Mama' was no longer young, and in any case had always disliked travelling and being away from the family hearth. She was also as sensitive to her son's needs as her husband was oblivious of them. It is abundantly clear from the evidence that Maria Anna was coerced into accompanying Mozart on his next journey, not as a solicitous caretaker but as a reluctant chaperone and informer. She was specifically instructed to report back to Leopold on Mozart's every association, especially with women. He even insisted that mother and son must share the same bedroom. Come what may, with Wolfgang's being sacked the

journey had now taken on the greatest urgency. It was more than *Mozart's mother*
ever imperative that he should find a stable and lucrative *Maria Anna,*
appointment. So mother and son left Salzburg with plenty of time *c. 1770*
to fit in several promising ports of call along the way.

Leopold's spirits as he bade them farewell could hardly have been lower, and the first reports from the travellers did nothing to lift them. For a start, the expected roles had been reversed. The son was the caretaker of the mother, as he revealed in a letter to his father:

Nothing comes amiss to me. I settled from the first to pay the coachmen and postilions, for I can talk to these fellows better than Mama. At the Stern, in Wasserburg, we are splendidly served; I am treated here like a prince. About half an hour ago the porter knocked at the door to take my orders about various things, and I gave them to him with the same grave air that I have in my portrait.

Nor was Maria Anna's first report what Leopold was in the mood to hear: 'We are leading the most enchanting life – up with the birds, to bed late at night, and visitors coming to see us from dawn till dusk. We live like the offspring of princes (until the hangman comes to fetch us)!' Leopold responded with the first of many increasingly stern reminders that they were travelling on his money, and all for the sake of his son. Reports of merrymaking and conviviality ceased immediately. In later, increasingly plaintive bulletins, Maria Anna left no doubt that she and Wolfgang could pinch pennies with the best of them:

I am at home, by myself, as usual, and have to tolerate the dreadful cold. Even if they light a small fire, they never come back to put more coal on, so the fire goes out, and the room is soon as cold as before. And even a little fire like this costs twelve kreuzer. So I have them light one in the morning, when we get up, and another in the evening. During the day I just have to shiver. Even now I can hardly hold my pen, since I am freezing so. Needless to say, we have not been to any balls and only to one play, for the tickets are far too expensive. And I seldom venture out of doors since I lack even an umbrella to protect me from the elements.

Mozart, on the other hand, was clearly enjoying himself, despite major disappointments in Munich, where the Elector had praised him lavishly while repeatedly stressing that there was no job going. 'No vacancy, dear boy. No vacancy!' Quite apart from the disappointment, the great composer was growing tired of being everyone's 'dear boy'. Nevertheless, he liked Munich, and was reluctant to leave it.

The travellers' next port of call was Augsburg, Leopold's birthplace. Although this was a short stopover – little more than a week, and a family visit rather than a scouting operation – Wolfgang gave two concerts, to the usual rapturous reception. Mozart's fame as a pianist makes it easy to forget that he was also a very fine violinist, especially during his teens, when he wrote all five of his violin concertos and often appeared as a soloist. After one particularly successful performance, he observed rather cryptically to Leopold, 'I played as though I were the greatest violinist in all Europe.' Yet as he grew into independent manhood, he seems to have lost interest in performing on the violin. From his early twenties onwards he confined his violin (and viola) playing to chamber music, made with friends in private.

It was in Augsburg that, for the first time since their early childhood, Wolfgang met his now eighteen-year-old cousin Maria Anna Thekla Mozart, known to the Salzburg Mozarts as 'the Bäsle' ('the little cousin'). He was clearly smitten:

> I must tell you, Papa, that she is beautiful, bright, high-spirited and as charming as can be. And we get on tremendously well, for, like me, she has a great sense of mischief. We both laugh at everyone and generally enjoy ourselves enormously.

It was perhaps the first time in his life that he had actually known a real playmate, and it brought out an aspect of his personality which confounded biographers throughout the nineteenth century and much of the twentieth. Part of it was an antic, off-the-wall sense of humour and an abandonment of all inhibition that shocked many a Victorian writer into an embarrassed silence. As he wrote to his cousin from Mannheim, a few weeks later:

> *O Heaven and hell! A thousand curses! Croatians and demons and witches and hags, the battalions of hell for eternity yell, by all of the elements (water and earth – and fire and air), Europe, America! Asia and Africa! Capucins, Jezwits! Franciscans, Dominicans! Augustinians, Benedictines, Carthusians and Minorites! Brothers of the Sacred Cross! Irrregular canons and regular too, all slackards and cowards and sluggards and knaves!! Higgledy-piggledy, asses and fools!!! Buffaloes, oxen, and nitwits and ghouls! What sort of behaviour is this, oh my dears? Four smart, snappy soldiers and three bandoliers!... Such a package to get, but no portrait as yet! So pray let me have it as quick as you can – and as I desired it, sexy and French!*

Then he changes tack, in a fashion typical of his letters to his cousin, but to no one else (with the surprising exception of his mother):

> *Forgive me my miserable scrawl, if you can, but my pen is already worn down to a shred, and I have been shitting, or so I am told, from birth to the present, through the same old hole, which isn't yet worn, not the tiniest whit, although I've been using it daily to shit, and each time the muck with my teeth I have bit.*

Another of his letters to her is dominated by obsessive repetitions of the words 'muck' and 'lick', while virtually all contain sexual and scatological innuendos based on various derivative rhymes. Curiously, this infantile fascination with excretion, licking, farting and so on seems to have been something of a family tradition. When his mother, the model of long-suffering gentility, wanted to cheer up her morose and self-pitying husband, she wrote to him shortly after leaving Salzburg: 'Keep well, my darling, my dear, my love. Into your mouth your ass you'll shove. I wish you good-night, my darling, but first: shit in your bed, and make it burst.'

As for Mozart's letters to the Bäsle, these are not all off-colour. In some, however, he seems to have taken leave of his senses:

> *Why not, I beg of you? – I must ask you, dearest dunce, why not?... Why should I not... beg Fraulein Josepha to forgive me for not having sent her the sonata?... Why not? – What? – Why not? – Why shouldn't I send it? – Why should I not it? – Why not? – Strange! I don't know why I shouldn't – So do me this favour – Why not? – Why should you not do it? – Why not? – Strange! I shall do the same for you, when you want me to. Why not? Why should I not do it, do it with you? Strange! Why not? – I cannot imagine why not? Why not?*

To do it, or not to do it. That was the question. And did they? It seems quite likely. Why else would he bother to reassure her, 'Since leaving you I have never taken my trousers off except before going to bed at night.' Whether they 'did' or 'didn't', there is no doubt at all that their feelings for each other went well beyond the physical. On the eve of his departure for Mannheim, Mozart wrote in her album: 'If you love that which I love, you will have to love yourself.' For her part, much of Mozart's attraction must surely have been the extraordinary contrast between the zany, earthy, exuberant young man as she came to know him very early on in their brief acquaintance and the genius who mesmerised audiences in the two concerts he gave in Augsburg.

When Mozart and his mother reached Mannheim at the end of October, the Bäsle was still much in his mind. When she asked, in a letter, how he liked it there, he replied, 'I like Mannheim as well as I can like any place where you are not.' Later in the same letter he wrote: 'If you can go on loving me as I love you, then our love will endure for all eternity.' Yet in Mannheim, probably to his own surprise, he lost his heart to someone even younger than the Bäsle.

Aloysia Weber, an exceptional soprano and an accomplished pianist, was only sixteen. But the combination of her voice, her talent and her considerable feminine charms was more than Mozart could resist. Indeed, he seems to have fallen in love with her entire family. Fridolin Weber, the father, was a former civil servant, now an impoverished musician and musical copyist, with a warm-hearted busybody of a wife and four daughters. At first all this was carefully concealed from Leopold; and any suspicions he harboured must have been allayed by his wife's reassurance that 'Our Wolfgang is kept so busy that he really has no idea whether he's standing on his head or his heels; between his composing and teaching (he gives a great many lessons) he has no time in which to socialise.' A letter from Mozart himself adds detail but gives roughly the same impression.

We can't very well get up much before eight o'clock, since our rooms, which are on the ground floor, get no daylight till eight-thirty. I then get dressed quickly and compose until midday, when I go over to Wendlings and compose a little more until half past one, when we break for lunch. At three, I go off to the Mainz Hotel to give a Dutch officer a lesson in thorough bass, but I have to be home again by four to instruct the daughter of the house, even though we can never really begin until half-past because the lights aren't brought in till then. At six I go to Cannabich's and give Mlle

Rosa her lesson, and then generally stay for supper, after which we
talk and sometimes make music.

Significantly, he makes no mention of the Webers. Mozart was indeed busy, but he certainly did have time to socialise. Freed from the hovering presence of his father, he quickly made many friends in Mannheim, most of whom, like Cannabich and Wendling, were musicians. Mannheim boasted at that time what may have been the finest orchestra in the world, and Cannabich was at its head. In the words of the celebrated Dr Burney, musician, writer and professional traveller: 'There are more solo players and good composers in this than perhaps in any other orchestra in Europe; it is an army of generals, equally fit to plan a battle as to fight it.' The Mannheim 'school' of composers comprised the leading pioneers in a new style of orchestral playing. Their trademark mannerism, generally at the start of a movement, was a vigorously rising arpeggio which came to be known as a 'Mannheim Rocket'. A famous example is the opening of the finale in Mozart's Symphony No. 40 in G minor.

As for Aloysia Weber, Mozart was undoubtedly in love with her. But the differences between the letters he wrote to the Bäsle and his one surviving letter to Aloysia could hardly be greater.

Dearest Friend!
I do beg your pardon for not sending the variations I have written
on the aria you sent me. But I felt it best to answer your father's
letter as soon as possible and thus have had no time in which to
write them out, but I promise you shall have them with my next
letter. I am hoping, as well, that my sonatas will soon be printed so
I can send them in the same package as the 'Popoli di Tessaglia',
which is already half finished. And if you like it half as much as I
do, I shall be more than content. In the meantime, until I know

Mozart with Aloysia Weber

*whether you really like it (and I desire no other praise than yours)
– I can only say that of all my compositions of this kind, this pleases
me the most. I shall also be most gratified if you will give your
concentrated attention to my Andromeda scene 'Ah, lo previdi,' for
I guarantee it will suit you well – and that you will do yourself
great credit with it. I must particularly advise you, however, to take
special care where the expression marks are concerned, to give
careful thought to the meaning and power of the words, to put
yourself as seriously as possible into Andromeda's situation and
position, to imagine, indeed, that you and she are one and the
same. With your beautiful voice, and your excellent manner of
producing it, you will undoubtedly become an excellent singer, and
very soon, if you continue to work as I advise.*

The tone of the letter is studiedly formal. Yet Mozart was so
much in love with Aloysia that he was prepared to abandon his
original plan to go on to Paris, as urged by Leopold, in order to
devote himself single-mindedly to her career. His first grand plan
was a trip to Italy, where, he assured her, he would use his power
and influence to help establish her at some prestigious opera
house. But he had not visited Italy for more than five years, and
his power and influence there were non-existent. The Webers,
moreover, knew perfectly well that Mozart was currently
unemployed and that the whole purpose of his present journey
was to secure for himself some suitable position. If the Webers
were sceptical, Leopold was thunderstruck. In the letter
announcing his change of itinerary, Wolfgang confessed: 'I am so
deeply attached to this wonderful but unfortunate family that my
fondest wish in life is to make them happy. With any luck I may
succeed.' In Leopold's reply we have one of the longest and most
extraordinary letters ever written by a father to his son: a single
paragraph of almost 4,000 words, of which these are only some
(for ease of reading, paragraphs have been introduced):

I have read your letter with unmitigated horror and astonishment. It has deprived me of a whole night's sleep. This morning I am so much weakened that the best I can do is to write very slowly, word by word. Until the present, God be praised, I have enjoyed the benefits of good health. But now? After this? Let me speak plainly. You know full well our tribulations in Salzburg; you know my wretched income, and all my other troubles; and you know why I agreed to let you go away. But let me repeat it. The aim of your journey was twofold: to win for yourself a good and permanent appointment, or, should you fail in this, to make your way in some big city where large quantities of money may be earned. Both these ends were designed to assist your parents and to help your dear sister. But it appears we are forgotten; now this other family is the most honourable, the most Christian family of your acquaintance, and the daughter is to have the leading role in the tragedy to be enacted between your true and rightful family and her own!

But towering above all this, the purpose of your trip was to build up your own name and reputation in the world. Part of this was achieved in your childhood and boyhood. Today, however, it rests with you alone to raise yourself to a level of eminence such as no musician has ever reached before. It now depends solely on your judgement and your mode of life whether you die as an ordinary musician, utterly forgotten, or as a famous Kapellmeister, whose name and work will be enshrined by posterity – whether, captured by some woman, you die on a bed of straw in an attic full of starving children, or whether, after a Christian life spent in contentment, honour and renown, you leave this world with your family well provided for and your name respected by all.

As for your current proposal (I can scarcely guide my trembling hand when I contemplate it) – this plan to gad about with Herr Weber, and, be it noted, his two daughters – it has almost deprived me of my sanity. How can you have been bewitched into entertaining such a grotesque idea even for an hour?! Quite apart from your own reputation, how could you think to expose your old father to the mockery and ridicule of the Prince and of the whole town which loves you? Yes, to expose me to mockery and yourself to contempt, for in answer to repeated appeals, I have already told everyone that you were going to Paris.

You proclaim yourself eager to spare me anxiety yet now overturn onto my head a whole bucketful of worries which are almost the end of me! You know that God in his goodness has given me sound judgement, and that in the most tortuous circumstances I have always, through my foresight, found ways of escape. What, then, has prevented you from seeking my counsel, and from always acting as I desired?

Your desire to help the oppressed comes straight from your father. But your first duty is to consider the well-being of your parents, or else your soul will be condemned to eternal damnation. Remember me now as you saw me last, standing beside the carriage in a state of the utmost wretchedness. Ill as I was, I had been packing for you late into the night, and there I was at the carriage again at six o'clock, seeing to everything for you. Hurt me now, if you can be so cruel! Win fame and make money in Paris – and when you have money to spend, then go off to Italy if you must. Your dear sister, incidentally, has wept copiously during these last two days. And who is accountable for that?! Off with you, then. To Paris. And soon!

Why to Paris? And why then? Because the Elector in Mannheim, like the Elector in Munich, despite his personal warmth to Mozart, had decided not to take him on. It would have been a crushing blow to Mozart in any case; but he was now more than ever attached to Mannheim, because Mannheim had Aloysia and her family, and Paris had not (a crucial part of Leopold's game plan). Mozart heard the unwelcome news not from the Elector himself but from one of his aides. His response was immediate:

I left the concert and went straightaway to see Madame Cannabich. The Treasurer, who is a good friend of mine, came with me. On the way I told him what had happened. He became wild beyond your imagining. When we came into the room, he instantly burst out: 'Well, here's another who has been favoured with the usual nice treatment they deal you out at Court.' 'What,' exclaimed Madame, 'so it has come to nothing?' I related the whole sorry tale, and in return they regaled me with accounts of many similar things which have occurred here. When Mademoiselle Rosa (who was in the third room from us, busy with the linen) had finished, she came in and said to me, 'Would you like me to start now?,' since it was time for her lesson. 'I am at your service!' said I. 'Do you know,' she said, quite innocently, 'that I mean to be very attentive today?' 'I am sure you will be,' answered I, 'for I'm afraid that our lessons won't go on for much longer.' 'How so?' says she. 'What do you mean? Why?' She turned to her Mama, who told her. 'What!?' she cried, 'is this really true? Oh I can't believe it.' 'Yes,' I replied, 'quite true, I'm afraid.' She then played my sonata, but looked very grave. And now I could not suppress my tears; in the end they all had tears in their eyes, for she was playing the sonata which is the favourite of the whole family, and whose slow movement is a portrait of Mlle Rosa herself.

Mozart had never wanted to go to Paris in the first place. With his heart now unexpectedly anchored in Mannheim, the French capital felt to him at times like a glorified prison. Mama's presence was no help either; nor was she any happier, as she revealed to Leopold:

As for my life here, it is irredeemably unpleasant. From morning till night I am cooped up here alone, I might as well be in jail. Our room is so dark and poorly situated that I don't catch even a glimpse of the sun all day, and the window looks out only onto a little courtyard. Unless it's raining I have no idea what the weather is like. I try to knit a little but the light is so poor and my fingers so cold that even that is a struggle. This room is cold even when the fire is on. As there is no clavier in our room, Wolfgang leaves early to go and work at the home of Monsieur Legros, the director of the Concert Spirituel, so I never see him all day long. If this goes on much longer I may forget entirely how to talk. But I must stop writing now, because my arm and eyes ache too much to continue.

Her husband's response to these lamentations was as chilly as that Parisian room. An immediate return to Salzburg was out of the question. As he continually pointed out, it was he who was footing the bill; and his plans, which he outlined with daunting clarity in a letter to his son, were not for Wolfgang alone:

If you could get a monthly salary from some prince in Paris, plus doing some work for concert series and the theatre, plus now and then having something engraved 'by subscription', and if your sister and I could give lessons and she could play at concerts and musical entertainments, then there should certainly be enough for us all to live in comfort.

Again and again, the stress is on the family unit, as if nothing had changed since the days of the childhood tours. Again and again he emphasises his dire financial straits, which he attributes entirely to his altruistic expenditure on his son's career. The guilt is piled on to Mozart layer after layer. The fact is that Leopold had made a fortune out of his children and had squirreled much of it away in various places, while continually complaining to others about his poverty. As a psychological strategist, Leopold could be a master.

If playing on Wolfgang's conscience over debt was the only means by which he could retain control of his son, then so be it:

You say you would like me to be more light-hearted in my letters. But you know that honour is dearer to me even than life. Consider the whole course of events. Remember that although I hoped you would help me to get out of debt, I have so far only sunk deeper and deeper. You know how high my credit has always been here – but if I lose that, I also lose my honour. And the Archbishop? Is he to have the satisfaction of gloating over our misfortune, and of being able to laugh at us and mock us? Rather than face this I would drop dead immediately.

Away in Paris, which he loathed, Mozart reassured his father:

I pray each day to God to grant me the strength and courage to hold out in this place, and to give me the honour of reflecting His immeasurably greater honour and glory; I pray that I am enabled to succeed here and earn large sums of money, so that I shall indeed be able to help you out of your troubles; and that He will allow us to meet again soon, so that we may live happily and contentedly together again. This is now my sole ambition.

Almost more shocking than Leopold's emotional blackmail is the real possibility that he had suppressed the best offer Mozart had yet received, and this before he had even left Salzburg. A vastly wealthy Viennese educator and philanthropist, Joseph Mesmer, had written to Leopold, saying that he was ready to provide Wolfgang with full room and board until a suitable position could be found for him. Some time later he followed this up with another letter:

Why did you not send your son directly to Vienna? And why do you hold back even now? As I have already told you, I can undertake to guarantee that all his needs shall be met free of charge, and that along with all your Viennese friends I shall strive tirelessly to secure some prestigious position for him. These things, however, can move slowly, as you well know, but there can be no doubt that Vienna is far the best place for him. Unless he is actually here, however, there is nothing to be done.

To give him credit, Leopold did eventually forward the letter to Mozart in Paris, adding that this gateway was still open to him – but advising him not to go through it.

Mozart made friends in Paris as easily as in other places. In general, though, he felt that the city, its traditions and its opportunities were incompatible with his own creative personality and outlook. Moreover, things did not look promising as regards the kind of appointment Leopold had in mind. He was far from idle, however. He took on some pupils and received commissions for a ballet (*Les Petits Riens*), a symphony, and a concerto for flute and harp – ironically, the only two instruments he professed to despise.

After the rebuffs in Munich and Mannheim, and his recent, turbulent correspondence with Leopold, Mozart's habit of obedience was coming under considerable strain. His first act of open rebellion was to refuse a highly prestigious and lucrative position which became vacant in May: the post of organist at the palace of Versailles. The list of reasons he gave his father was convincing enough, but incomplete. It was also not entirely truthful.

As far as Versailles is concerned, after talking it over with good friends who really know the scene here, I have decided to decline the post, which in any case doesn't pay particularly well. And for half of every year I should have to moulder away in a place where there are no opportunities at all for other ways of making one's living and where my talent would hardly count for anything. To

*enter the service of the King in Versailles, according to the best
authorities, is to be as good as forgotten in Paris. Of course I would
love to have the honour of a really good appointment, but it must
be as a well-paid Kapellmeister, not as a mere organist.*

What he neglects to say is that he disliked Paris anyway, that he
came there unwillingly, that along with its other shortcomings it
lacked Aloysia, and that he wished he had remained in
Mannheim. His comments on the first rehearsal for his new
symphony, however, were unsparing:

*I have written a symphony for the opening of the Concert
Spirituel. I felt very edgy at the rehearsal, because I have never
heard a worse performance. You can't imagine how twice over
they scraped and scrambled through it. I was frankly in a terrible
state and would have loved to have had it rehearsed again, but I
was told there was no more time. So I went to bed with an aching
heart and in a very disgruntled and indignant mood. The next
morning I made up my mind not to go to the concert at all; but in
the evening, since the weather was fine, I had second thoughts and
decided to go, after all. But I was determined that if the symphony
went as badly as it had during the rehearsal, I would walk
straight into the orchestra, snatch the violin from Lahoussaye, the
concertmaster, and conduct the piece myself!*

In the event, there was no need. The performance came off well,
and the symphony was rapturously received. Mozart's account of
the occasion, however, gives cause to be grateful that the
'authenticist' movement of our own time has not seen fit to
encourage the revival of eighteenth-century-style audiences:

*Just in the middle of the first movement there is a passage which I
felt sure would find favour. But little could I have guessed how*

right I was. The audience were so carried away that there was a tremendous burst of applause, right in the middle of the movement. But since I knew, when I wrote it, the effect it was likely to produce, I had introduced the passage again at the close – when there were shouts of 'Encore! Encore!'

The audience participation evidently extended to both ends of the dynamic spectrum:

Having observed that all last as well as first Allegros begin here with all the instruments playing at once and generally in unison, I began mine with two violins only, piano *for the first eight bars – immediately followed by a* forte; *the audience, exactly as I expected, said 'hush' at the quiet beginning, and when they heard the* forte, *immediately started to applaud again.*

After the concert, Mozart celebrated its success in his own fashion. As he wrote to Leopold:

I was so happy with the performance that as soon as it was over, I went off to the Palais Royal, where I had a large ice cream, said the Rosary as I had sworn I would, and went home – for as you know, I am always, and shall always be happiest there, or else in the company of some good, upright German who, if he is a bachelor, lives alone like a true Christian, or, if married, loves his wife and brings up his children properly.

Mozart, it seems, was still very much in the business of currying favour with Papa. By the time Leopold reached this part of the letter, however, he was probably past caring – for the moment. All the Parisian extracts quoted above derive from a letter which begins very differently:

My dearest, dear Father,

I'm afraid I have very sad and upsetting news to give you. My dear mother is gravely ill. She has been bled, as in the past, and it was very necessary too. She felt better afterwards, but only a few days later she became feverish, along with shivering, headache and diarrhoea. To begin with we used the usual home remedies, but as she got steadily worse (she could hardly speak and her hearing deteriorated very rapidly, so that I had to shout to make myself understood) Baron Grimm sent us his doctor. But she is feverish and delirious, and very weak. They say there's hope – but it doesn't look that way to me. I have been hovering day and night between hope and fear – but I have resigned myself entirely to the will of God – and I pray that you and my dear sister will do the same.

The truth of it, as Leopold probably guessed, is that she was already dead. The letter, which goes on, at great length, to ramble through all kinds of news and gossip as though nothing was amiss, was written within a few hours of her death. Later came the details:

In the final hour of her earthly life, she was unconscious – her life flickered out like a candle. Three days before, she had made her confession, partaken of the Sacrament and received Extreme Unction. Almost from then on, however, she was completely delirious, and at twenty-one minutes past five o'clock she lost all sensation and consciousness. I gripped her hand in mine and spoke to her – but she neither saw nor heard me. All feeling was gone. Thus she lay, now more dead than alive, until she breathed her last, five hours later. No one was present but myself, a kind friend of mine, Herr Heina, and the nurse. The memory of this dreadful experience will be with me to the end of my days. You know that I had never seen anyone die. How cruel that the first occasion should have been the death of my own mother. At that moment I wished for nothing but to follow her. Weep. Weep your fill, as I have done, but find consolation in the knowledge that it was the will of Almighty God. Let us, therefore, say a heartfelt Paternoster for her soul and turn our thoughts to other matters, for all things have their proper time.

Then, as before, he turned his thoughts to other matters.

Mozart's capacity for detachment – and there are many examples of it – easily gives an impression of insensitivity. Years later he would calmly compose while his wife was in labour with their first child in the next room. Contrary to popular belief, there is no guarantee that the character of a composer's music will match the circumstances surrounding its composition. It seems probable, nevertheless, that the slow movement of Mozart's A minor Piano Sonata, K.310, with its anguished middle section, is a truer reflection of his inner state than his rambling letter to Leopold. Letter and music, roughly contemporaneous, derive from the same source: a twenty-two-year-old, in an uncongenial foreign city, who has never been apart from one or other of his parents for more than a day or two. He is the only member of his family to have seen his mother dead – to have seen her actually die; and he has to look after all the arrangements. In these circumstances he receives a letter from his father, whose mind seems bent on one conclusion:

I told you as long ago as May that your mother should be bled, yet it was put off until 11 June, and even then she was probably bled too little; and finally, you summoned the doctor far too late, when it was perfectly clear that she was mortally ill. But you had your engagements, you left her alone all day, and since she didn't make a fuss, you treated the matter far too lightly. During all this time her illness grew steadily worse. And where were you?

This, however, is only the overture. Leopold now further twists the knife, suggesting, by implication, that Mozart had doomed his mother in the very act of being born: 'Well, it's all over now,' he writes. 'God willed it. The unbreakable chain of Divine Providence saved your mother's life when you were born, at which time we thought that her hour had come. But no. She was fated to sacrifice herself for her son in a different way.' Now the son was to sacrifice himself for his father. Having failed in his mission, thrown away his chances at Versailles, and negligently disposed of his mother, not to mention dallying with Aloysia, Mozart was duty-bound to return to Salzburg – so Leopold argued. To sugar the pill, Leopold regaled his son with a list of the privileges and advantages that would await him there. Mozart was unmoved. Among the many arguments against this plan, he cited one with uncharacteristic venom: 'I must tell you that one of the chief reasons for my hatred of Salzburg is those coarse, slovenly, dissipated court musicians, amongst whom no honest man of good breeding could possibly live!!' Mozart too, it seems, could twist the knife:

Instead of being happy to mix with them, he must feel ashamed of their very company. This is probably why musicians are both unloved and disrespected with us. Ah, but if the orchestra were only run on the same lines as in Mannheim! If only you could see the order that prevails there: the unquestioned authority vested in Cannabich; the seriousness and dedication of the musicians. Cannabich, far and away the finest director known to me, is both beloved and feared by his troops, who, like himself, are held in the highest respect by the whole town. And oh how differently they comport themselves! They have good manners! They dress well – and do not go to taverns for the express purpose of getting drunk. Unless the Prince will place his trust in either you or me, and grant us full powers, which are essential requirements for any proper conductor, such conditions will never prevail in Salzburg. If I were to undertake such a role in Salzburg, I should have to be granted total authority. The Grand Chamberlain should have no say whatever in musical matters, or on any point relating to music. Not everyone in authority can become a Kapellmeister, but a Kapellmeister must become a person of authority. Even if my every point was agreed to, however, which you will admit is hardly likely, the fact remains that I would rather be anywhere than Salzburg.

Sugaring the pill was now abandoned as Leopold duly returned to form:

I am now in deep trouble. My debts now run to about 700 florins and I have not the slightest notion how I am going to support myself and your sister on my miserable monthly salary. It must be as clear as a cloudless sky to you that the future of your old father and your loving sister now rests entirely in your hands.

Leopold was actually still in his fifties, though one would hardly guess it from his letters:

I am elderly, and God may call me to Him at any time. But on no account will I die in debt... I will not have it that in order to pay off my creditors our things will be wretchedly sold once I am gone!... It is only with your salary that I can be certain of paying off everything in a few years so that I may be able to die in peace: and that I must and that I will. If, when you come home, you do not lift this weighty burden from my heart, it will crush me utterly. God willing, I would like to live a few years longer, and make good my debts – and then, should you care to do so, you can run your head against the wall. But I am sick and tired of writing these lengthy letters to you. In the last year and more I have practically written myself blind.

Under an onslaught of letters like these, Mozart's resolve to hold his own began to crumble:

> *MOZART: I'm sorry, but I really cannot write any more now, for my heart overflows with tears. I hope you will write to me soon and comfort me.*

> *LEOPOLD: You say that I ought to comfort you? I say, come and comfort me!*

It comes as no surprise by now to learn that Mozart sank into periods of deep depression. His mother's death alone would have seen to that. But that began to seem the least of it. 'I often wonder whether my life is even worth going on with. I feel neither hot nor cold – I am numbed, and cannot find much pleasure in anything.' But Leopold was in no mood to take such confessions seriously. 'You were obviously feeling disgruntled or irritated at the time. You were clearly writing in a bad humour. I must tell you, I don't like it.' For Leopold, it seemed, the problem was simply solved: 'Once you have made your father's happiness your first priority, *then* will he continue to think of your welfare and happiness and to stand by you as a loyal friend.'

The longer Mozart held out, the more Leopold tightened the screws: 'I hope, after your mother had to die so inappropriately in Paris, that you will not also have the hastening of your *father's* death upon your conscience.' He reinforced his point in a letter written shortly afterwards: 'If you continue to stay away, I shall die much sooner. You alone can save me from death.'

Such was Mozart's reluctance to go home that he stayed on in Paris long after his mother's death, and grew so short of money that he pawned her watch. In the meantime Leopold secured for his son a position as court organist at Salzburg – the post he had spurned at Versailles. Mozart finally surrendered. On his leisurely journey home he called in at Mannheim, only to find that the court, and with it the Webers, had decamped to Munich. On his arrival in Munich, Aloysia, who almost certainly never reciprocated his feelings, and was now involved with another man, coldly rebuffed him. Before he continued on his way he reopened his correspondence with the Bäsle, who joined him in Munich and accompanied him to Salzburg. Here she was probably coolly received by Leopold as well as Nannerl, who now took her father's side in everything. In any case, the relationship between Mozart and the Bäsle was never the same again, and she effectively drops out of the story altogether.

Journey 3: 1777–9

Origin: Salzburg **(1)**

1777

Munich **(2)**   Mozart fails to secure a position and moves on to his father's home town.

Augsburg **(3)**   Befriends his cousin Maria Thekla Mozart ('the Bäsle') and gives dazzling concert.

1778

Mannheim **(4)**   Falls in love with Aloysia Weber and to Leopold's horror decides to cancel projected visit to Paris; Leopold's will, however, prevails.

Paris **(5)**   His mother dies; he composes, among other things, Concerto for flute and harp, K.299, Symphony in D, K.297 ('Paris') and Violin Sonata in E minor, K.304. Finding no position, he begins reluctantly to make his way home.

Strasbourg **(6)**   Gives private concert with great success, but few attend his public concert.

Mannheim **(7)**   Hopes to see the Webers, but finds they have decamped with the court to Munich.

Munich **(8)**   He is rebuffed by Aloysia but renews his friendship with the Bäsle.

1779

Salzburg **(9)**   Returns home in mid-January 1779, accompanied by the Bäsle, to a life he characterises as a form of 'slavery'.

Interlude IV:
Symphonies and Concertos

The Symphonies

Mozart wrote his first symphony in 1764, when he was eight, and his last, the so-called 'Jupiter', in 1788. Of all those that came in between, none is less than attractive. It was not until 1773, however, when he was seventeen, that he wrote one which could conceivably be called a major work. In its inner turbulence and passion, Symphony No. 25 in G minor was something new. Here, for the first time in his symphonies, we encounter a voice which is unmistakably individual. This is a composer speaking directly from his inner self, expressing emotions which he knows from first-hand experience, and handling his musical material with the skill of a master. No allowances need be made for his age. The next major work in the sequence, written a year later, is Symphony No. 29 in A: happy, serene, tender, buoyant, brilliantly energetic and captivating in its sound-world. Even more than its G minor predecessor, the symphony is an astonishing achievement for a composer still in his teens. It is all the more surprising, then, that in 1778, responding to his son's request for some scores in Paris, Leopold advised him to withhold this and other symphonies from publication:

It is better that whatever does you no honour should not be given to the public. That is the reason why I have not given any of your symphonies to be copied, because I suspect that when you are older and have more insight, you will be glad that no one has got hold of them, though at the time you composed them you were quite pleased with them. One gradually becomes more and more fastidious.

No honour? When you are older? More insight? More fastidious? Never before, as far as we know, had Leopold taken this disapproving, condescending tone about his son's music. Perhaps, though, we should not be surprised. Leopold had only relatively recently been faced with works in which the son so decisively eclipses the father. Artistically speaking, 'Papa', after God or otherwise, had been proved entirely redundant. His job was done. With three works in particular — the G minor Symphony, K.183, the E flat Piano Concerto, K.271 (see pp. 94-5), and this entrancing A major Symphony — Mozart had moved decisively into the ranks of the great.

The next landmark symphony, No. 31 in D, was composed in the French capital, and has borne the nickname 'Paris' ever since. Specifically tailored to the French taste, it marks the first appearance of clarinets in Mozart's symphonies (there were none in Salzburg at that time). Otherwise, and perhaps predictably, this is not one of Mozart's most winning scores. For the next great symphonies, we leapfrog over Nos 32, 33 and 34 to arrive at the final six, all written after his move to Vienna in 1781. It is overwhelmingly these — No. 35 in D, the so-called 'Haffner', No. 36 in C (the 'Linz'), No. 38 in D (the 'Prague'), No. 39 in E flat, No. 40 in G minor, and No. 41 in C (the 'Jupiter') — that have ensured Mozart's immortality as a symphonist. In their perfection of form, variety of character, individuality of tone and emotional and spiritual reach, they are like nothing written before them, not even by Haydn. The last three were composed, astonishingly, in the space of six weeks and at a time of mounting financial desperation. It seems inconceivable that Mozart knew they were to be his last symphonies. He was only thirty-two and still had three years to live. But they undoubtedly sum up everything he had learned as a symphonist, and had a major influence on the subsequent development of symphonic thought. In their inspired yet methodical use of orchestral textures to expressive ends (especially their 'liberation' of the wind instruments), in their harmonic power and range, and in their characterisation and development of themes, they expanded a form which had previously been rather slight into one of the monumental achievements of the human mind.

The Concertos

In no field, not even the opera and the symphony, was Mozart's legacy more epoch-making than in the realm of the concerto. In the case of both the symphony and the string quartet, Haydn's contribution was as great as Mozart's. In opera, there was the great reformer Gluck, who died only four years before Mozart. In the case of the concerto there was only Mozart. It seems only right, then, that this branch of his output should take pride of place in this survey.

Like Beethoven's sonatas and Bach's fugues, Mozart's concertos serve as a kind of diary of his entire creative life. His first concertos, as noted in Interlude II, were actually arrangements of solo piano pieces by other composers. Even when not overtly dramatic, Mozart's works are almost invariably musical conversations. But it is specifically in the world of musical theatre that we find the true models for Mozart's concertos. Mozart's great concertos are in many ways like operas without words, alive with sparkling dialogues, dramatic confrontations, acute psychological insights and unforgettable characterisations. His melodies, and what happens to them, are remarkably like the characters in his operas. He was the first composer to re-create in instrumental terms the dramatic traditions of musical theatre at its finest. What makes his achievement still more miraculous is that he did it all within more or less pre-ordained forms.

His first entirely original concerto, the Piano Concerto in D, K.175, was written in 1773, when he was seventeen, and already it left even the best of his contemporaries (Haydn excepted) in the shade. Many of its first listeners, however, were startled by its sophistication of style, culminating in a finale full of masterful counterpoint which made unusual 'intellectual' demands of the audience. Today, one can only wonder what the fuss was about. Still, Mozart took it to heart and in 1782 replaced it with a charming but undemanding Rondo, K.382. The concerto is rarely performed today except as part of the complete cycle.

Passing over the Bassoon Concerto and the slight and rarely heard *Concertone* for two violins of 1774, the five violin concertos – all but the first (1773) dating from 1775 – are the earliest of his concertos to find a permanent place in the concert repertoire. They were probably all intended for his own performance, at Salzburg, and are as elegant as anything he ever wrote. Entertaining, brilliant, touching, deliciously spiced and perfectly proportioned, they contain such an abundance and variety of inspired melody that there sometimes seems room for little else. But who's to complain? All the violin concertos are gems in their different ways, but one No. 5 in A major – stands out above all the others and remains one of the most popular concertos ever written. Because of the 'exotic' A minor episode in the last movement, the work has become known as the 'Turkish' Concerto.

The next three concertos, two for solo piano (K.238 and K.246), one (K.242) for three pianos, are neither major works nor particularly significant, but are entirely enjoyable nevertheless.

With the Piano Concerto No. 9 in E flat, K.271, however, composed in 1777, Mozart effectively broke the sound barrier. Indeed, the concerto can be seen as his own declaration of independence, the work with which he came of age. In its breathtaking originality and unprecedented emotional range, it remains one of the most significant concertos in the history of the genre. As such, it deserves special attention.

From the second bar it must have made every member of its first-night audience snap to attention as if they had all been given an electric shock. No sooner is the chordal fanfare of the opening bar concluded than the soloist enters, breaking with the practice of every concerto written up to that time and completing the opening phrase. After a brief, good-natured tug-of-war, the piano then retreats while the orchestra gets on with the business of the 'real' exposition. When the piano re-enters the fray it again breaks with tradition by coming in several bars early, while the orchestra is still playing, with a long anticipatory trill. From the beginning, and for the first time in the history of the medium, soloist and orchestra appear as equal partners in a genuine dialogue which continues throughout the work. This break with the past is symbolic as well as musical. The old melody-and-accompaniment approach to concerto writing, as in other spheres of music, was a perfect mirror of the stratified society in which a wealthy aristocracy held sway over the far more numerous populace of its subordinates (Haydn, for example, wore a servant's livery for most of his creative life, even when he enjoyed international fame). The rise of an affluent middle class, however, rendered this scheme of things increasingly untenable; and notions of democracy soon conferred unprecedented rights on the individual within society at large. Absolutism gave way to social structures which could achieve equilibrium only through a measure of compromise and accommodation on all sides. So it was in music.

It seems appropriate that Mozart, the first great composer after Handel to exchange the shackles of patronage for the life of the freelance, should be the first to liberate orchestra and soloist alike and let them engage in continuous conversation. The level and the nature of the dialogue in K.271 were unprecedented. So, too, was the promotion of the wind section (oboes and horns) to the front ranks of musical diplomacy (the dialogue between oboe and piano in the opening *Allegro* was the first of many such charming exchanges). From now on in his concertos, with only a few exceptions, Mozart gives the wind band a dual role: as a magical blending agent in his orchestral palette, and as a mediator between the soloist and the rest of the orchestra. The integration of the one amongst the many, the combining of parts into a greater whole, was one of Mozart's greatest achievements.

Nowhere is the close connection between opera and concerto more evident, or more powerfully expressed, than in the slow movement of this amazing work, replete with profound arioso passages and even recitatives (see Glossary). Nor had Mozart ever achieved a more subtle and telling use of tone colour (one of the most consistent features of all his concertos). The final movement is both topical and prophetic. Like many of his other finales, it adheres, if sometimes rather loosely, to the form of a rondo, then all the rage amongst continental music lovers. The main theme, a duple-metre *Presto* of tremendous energy, is among the most exciting Mozart ever wrote; but what singles the movement out for special comment is the interpolation in its midst of an extended episode in triple metre, marked 'Menuetto cantabile'. The abrupt change of mood, texture, tempo and metre retains its delicious shock value even today.

Next in the line of great concertos comes the Concerto in E flat for two pianos, K.365 of 1780, a sparkling virtuoso entertainment, with just a hint, in the slow movement, of darker, deeper regions. Written for Mozart and his sister to play, it must surely top the concerto repertoire of every duo-piano team in the world. Far greater in scope is the emotionally profound *Sinfonia concertante* in E flat, K.364 for violin, viola and orchestra, written in the same year. Its seriousness is evident from the very beginning. With the exception of K.271, this is by general consent Mozart's greatest instrumental work to date. Unlike the Concerto for two pianos, the soloists here are easy to distinguish, the viola having a special tone colour of its own, as well as being at a lower pitch. This makes the sustained conversation between the two soloists all the clearer – but the conversation is of two kinds. Often it follows the age-old pattern of 'call and response' (in which a 'statement' by one soloist is followed by an 'answer' from the other), or the two soloists may celebrate their unity by joining together in simultaneous 'song' (only in music can two or more voices speak at the same time and actually enhance the sense of what is being said). As in all Mozart's concertos, there are also frequent interchanges between soloists and orchestra.

When Mozart returned to the solo concerto in 1782, he had married and embarked on a freelance career in Vienna. To this end he composed three piano concertos (K.413, K.414, K.415) avowedly aimed at captivating amateur and connoisseur alike; and to ensure maximum sales in the domestic market, he so designed them that the wind parts could be dispensed with for performance a *quattro* – though K.415 in C loses much without its ceremonial trumpets and drums.

The wind parts (oboes and horns) are also optional in the E flat Piano Concerto, K.449 of 1784, though in every other sense it stands apart both from its predecessors and from its five companions of the same year (K.450, K.451, K.453, K.456 and K.459). One of Mozart's subtlest exercises in controlled ambiguity, it hovers unsettlingly between vivacity and turmoil, contrapuntal severity and spontaneous expression. As he recognised himself, it is quite unlike anything else he had written to date. (Interestingly too, it became the first work entered in the private catalogue of his works which he began in 1784 and continued until his death.) Mozart's concertos, like Beethoven's sonatas, are not least remarkable for their extraordinary diversity. While they share certain superficial resemblances, each explores musical problems and spiritual expression in a manner peculiar to itself. If this E flat Concerto gives us Mozart at his most concentrated and inwardly searching, its two immediate successors, K.450 in B flat and K.451 in D, reveal him at his most public and self-confident. Both can be numbered among the most technically challenging works he ever wrote, and both, especially K.451, reflect the impact of his friendship with Haydn.

Also indebted to Haydn are the four horn concertos, which are among the shortest and most instantly accessible that Mozart composed – hence their perennial popularity. Written for his friend Joseph Leutgeb (see pp. 53–4), they are suitably uncomplicated and outdoorsy, with echoes of the hunt never far away.

Nowhere in Mozart's concertos is the influence of Haydn heard to better or richer effect than in the two numerical siblings of 1785, the brooding D minor Piano Concerto, K.466 – still the most famous of all Mozart's concertos – and the dazzling C major, K.467, whose first movement is based almost entirely on the spare outlines of its opening march-like theme. Of all Mozart's slow movements, none seems to have exercised a greater spell on modern listeners than the *Andante* of this C major Concerto. It does not matter that the catalyst here was the soft-focus, sentimental Swedish film *Elvira Madigan* from 1967. Many more people have come to know and love this movement than ever saw the film, and record companies have shamelessly attached the name of the film to the concerto. Where we today find only beauty of the most haunting, pleasurably searing kind, Leopold Mozart was alarmed by the dissonances which so enhance its spell. The wonderful E flat Piano Concerto, K.482 of 1785 is less densely

argued, but no work of Mozart's can surpass it for grandeur of conception (though K.503 is its equal) or ravishing deployment of instrumental colour. The interpolation of what is in effect an extra slow movement in the midst of the finale (shades of K.271) is a poetic masterstroke.

Like the preceding year, 1786 saw the birth of three sharply contrasting piano concertos. The lyrical warmth of No. 23 in A major, K.488, and the poignancy of its F sharp minor *Adagio* (Mozart's only movement in this key), have made it a favourite with generations of music lovers. No. 24 in C minor, K.491 is unique in many respects, not least for the abiding sense of darkness with which it ends. Even the stormy D minor, No. 20, K.466, had finished on a note of optimism; but here Mozart's increasing awareness that he had grown beyond the reach of his Viennese audience keeps its grip on the piece from beginning to end. Who, then, would expect that his next essay in the medium would be the most symphonic and Olympian affirmation of the life force in the entire canon? The C major Concerto, K.503 is the culmination (though not the end) of the composer's long journey in the realm of the concerto. Here is the apotheosis of that final union of form and content, of symphony, concerto and opera, towards which he had been striving since his first tentative explorations.

The remaining two piano concertos represent, between them, an elegant attempt to regain public favour and a new departure. Not even its most sympathetic champions would claim that the so-called 'Coronation' Concerto, K.537 gives us Mozart at his best. Nevertheless, it was for many years among his most popular works, and only in recent decades has it become fashionable to denigrate it. The nickname, derived from Mozart's intention to perform it at the coronation of Leopold II in October 1790, evokes unflattering comparisons with Beethoven's 'Emperor'. But the work has many virtues, and reveals new subtleties on repeated hearings.

Mozart's last concerto for the piano, K.595 in B flat, has taken on valedictory associations nurtured by the wisdom of hindsight. It is hardly possible, however, that the thirty-four-year-old composer saw it as his farewell to the medium. With its apparent simplicity of utterance, its transcendence of earthly storms and stresses, and its breathtaking economy of means, the concerto simultaneously closes one chapter and opens what Mozart had every reason to believe was another.

There was one more concerto to come, however: the great, autumnal Clarinet Concerto in A, K.622, finished in October 1791 when Mozart was terminally ill. This is not only his last concerto, but his last major completed work, and it finds him at the height of his powers. Ironically, the man for whom he wrote both this and the equally wonderful Clarinet Quintet, was in a small way responsible for Mozart's circumstances. Despite his own money troubles, Mozart had for some time been giving financial assistance to his friend Anton Stadler, one of the foremost clarinettists of the day. Stadler, for his part, not only accepted the cash but went on to cheat his benefactor; yet Mozart's affection and admiration for him seem never to have waned.

Mozart's orchestral writing in this final work is a marvel in itself. Everything favours the mellow tone of the clarinet – which is supported by the usual body of strings, complemented by a wind group in which oboes (whose sharp, penetrating sound would have clashed with the soloist) have been replaced by flutes – and here again we find Mozart writing lovingly for an instrument he once claimed to despise.

Mozart transformed the concerto, and the piano concerto in particular, almost beyond recognition. In place of the stereotyped virtuoso vehicle and the urbane conversation piece cultivated by even the best composers of the rococo like J.C. Bach, Mozart left a form in which subtle tonal variety played a prime part in the cohesion of large-scale structures. He created a tapestry of interweaving strands in which unity was achieved through continuous diversity; an instrumental drama as eloquent and various as any opera. Above all he conjured a Utopian vision of a world without victors and vanquished, a 'republic of equals', to borrow a phrase from Schumann, in which altruism and self-interest are so intimately linked as to become indistinguishable.

Coda: Miscellaneous Orchestral Music

Lying midway between Mozart's symphonies and his concertos, though not attaining quite the exalted heights of either, are nine large-scale orchestral works, to which Mozart seems interchangeably to have given the name Serenade or, less frequently, Cassation. They were all designed originally for performance in the open air during the fine months of summer, and were invariably connected with a social event. The great 'Haffner' Serenade, K.250, for instance, was written to celebrate a marriage in Salzburg's prominent Haffner family, and was first played on the evening before the wedding. The serenades are multi-movement works, some having as many as seven or eight, and often begin with a slow introduction (a rarity in Mozart's symphonies). Often, too, they contain concerto-like movements, usually featuring a solo violin – as in the early Cassation in G, K.63 and, most famously, the 'Haffner' Serenade. Some, like the 'Haffner' and the so-called 'Posthorn' Serenade, K.320, are major works (featuring in the latter case double wind band, strings, trumpets and drums); others, like the celebrated *Eine kleine Nachtmusik*, K.525, are relatively small-scale and intimate. Indeed, *Eine kleine Nachtmusik* was conceived as chamber music, although it is often performed today by a chamber orchestra. The same is true of a number of Mozart's divertimentos, all of which were written as chamber music, with one instrument per part. Outstanding among these is the irresistible Divertimento in D,

Manuscript extract of Mozart's Eine kleine Nachtmusik

K.334, with its soloistic first violin part. There are also a few related one-offs, of which the most striking and original is the haunting, dark-toned Masonic Funeral Music, with its unique scoring of two oboes, three basset-horns, double bassoon, two horns and strings.

Chapter 5

Marriage, Money and
Paternity

Marriage, Money and Paternity

Once reunited in Salzburg in January 1779, Mozart and his father regained something of their former closeness. For the next eighteen months or so, however, the composer led a spectacularly uneventful life in his native city. As a salaried church organist, choirmaster and instructor of choirboys, he was as overqualified as J.S. Bach had been in a similar capacity. His immersion in composing when not otherwise occupied must have been both an escape route from the humdrum social life and an almost desperate determination to follow the vocation for which he felt he had been put on this earth. During this period he wrote some of his finest choral music, including the 'Coronation' Mass in C, K.317, and the *Vesperae solennes de confessore*, K.339.

But Mozart was always a man of the theatre, and Salzburg's lack of adequate facilities grated on his nerves. It was a matter of great excitement, then, when in the summer of 1780 he received a commission to write a new opera for Munich. The result was his first undoubted operatic masterpiece, *Idomeneo*. But though it was well received at its opening, it ran for only three performances: a casualty of timing. While written for the carnival season, the onset of Lent precluded further performances. Also significant is a review in a Munich newspaper, which waxed lyrical about the scenery, paused briefly to note that 'the text, music and translation are all by natives of Salzburg', but neglected to name the composer! Particularly disappointing for Mozart was the lack of interest shown by the Elector, despite having praised the opera to all and sundry after attending one of the rehearsals.

The Archbishop had not seen fit to come to Munich for his employee's opera but had taken up temporary residence in Vienna, where he now required Mozart's attendance. To his employer's annoyance, Mozart lost no opportunity to promote himself and cultivate useful contacts. Among these was the influential Countess Thun. As Mozart reported to Leopold, 'I've had lunch with her twice already, and hardly a day goes by without my calling on her. She is quite the most charming and lovable lady I have ever had the honour to know, and *she* regards *me* with the very highest favour.' It certainly made a change from lunching at the Archbishop's:

> There, we eat, as a rule, around noon, rather too early for me, but what can one do? Our group consists of the two valets, the Archbishop's private messenger, the confectioner, two cooks – and my insignificant self. The two valets have their place at the top of the table but at least I have the great privilege of being seated above the cooks.

Despite attempts by the Archbishop to block him, Mozart became well acquainted with the Viennese musical establishment and gave one or two high-profile concerts, which promptly became the talk of the town. He also discovered, to his delight, that the Webers had moved to Vienna. Aloysia was now married and expecting her first child, but they met again as friends, the rebuff at Munich forgotten. Fridolin had died, and his widow now lived with Aloysia's three unmarried sisters. This happy reunion, his new acquaintance with members of the aristocracy, and the warmth of his reception by the Viennese public all brought to a head Mozart's long-simmering frustration with his situation in Salzburg:

Three times already this gracious Prince-Archbollocks has said the most insulting and impertinent things to my face, which I shall not repeat, as I wish to spare your feelings, and it was only because I always had you, my dear father, before my eyes that I didn't take my revenge right then and there. He called me a knave and a dissolute cad and other injurious names, and told me to clear off. Then it all came out, as in a single breath, that I was the most dissipated scoundrel he knew, no man had ever served him so badly, and he threatened to write home and stop my salary if I failed to remove myself forthwith. It was impossible for me to get in a single syllable, for his words blazed away like a fire. He called me a scoundrel, a villain, a rogue and other such delicate bouquets. Finally, I could restrain myself no longer, and I said, 'Your Grace is not satisfied with me?' 'How dare you threaten me, you miserable, dim-witted little louse?' he replied. 'There is the door, and I tell you I shall have nothing more to do with such scum!' At last I said, 'Nor I with you!' 'Then be off,' says he, 'scram, get out of my sight!' Before I was quite out of the room I retorted, 'That's it. This is the end! You shall have it in writing in the morning.'

But it was not the end. There was one more ugly scene, this time with the Archbishop's chamberlain, in which Mozart was literally booted out of the room with a kick on his backside. Technically speaking, however, he had not been fired. He had resigned. On 8 June 1781, at the age of twenty-five, he felt free for the first time in his life. Leopold was appalled, commanding his son to recant and beg for reinstatement, as he himself had once done. Wolfgang was incredulous:

You say the only way I can preserve my honour is to go back on my resolve? How can you possibly perpetrate such a suggestion?!... It's common knowledge that my honour was insulted... Are you seriously proposing that I represent myself as a cowardly worm and the Archbishop a worthy prince?... You say, unbelievably, that as I have never shown you the slightest affection, the moment has now come for me to do so. Can this really be you? And then to suggest that I would never think of sacrificing any of my pleasures for the sake of my father? What pleasures do you suppose I have here? Can you seriously believe that I am revelling in pleasures and amusements... Dearest, most beloved father, I beg of you, do not ask me to recant. Ask of me anything, but not that – anything but that – the very thought of it makes me shake with rage.

He did not recant. Whatever the risks – and he knew them – he was free from servitude. Free for the first time in his life to be the arbiter of his own fate, or so he then believed. To begin with, things went well for him. He was busy playing concerts, composing, teaching, and Vienna's most important music publisher, Artaria, agreed to publish his compositions. Then, within weeks of his liberation from the servants' table, he received a major commission for a new opera, *The Abduction from the Seraglio*. On Christmas Eve, in the presence of the Emperor, he had his famous pianistic duel with the Italian composer-pianist Muzio Clementi. One of the greatest and most influential virtuosos in pianistic history, Clementi led off with his Sonata in B flat, Op. 24 No. 2, whose opening Mozart later pinched for his *Magic Flute* Overture. Mozart then weighed in with an improvisation and a set of variations. When the contestants retired to their respective corners, the Emperor pronounced his verdict: 'Clementi has only art. Mozart has art and taste.'

As the new year of 1782 dawned, Mozart, now nearly twenty-six, stood on the brink of the second greatest decision of his life. Even before his resignation, he had moved in with the Webers. For Leopold, deeply suspicious of women in general, the thought of his son ensnared in the home of a widow and her three unmarried daughters was predictably alarming. He somehow got wind of rumours that Mozart was contemplating marriage with one of the daughters, and wrote to his son in horror. Mozart, however, dismissed the rumours as nonsense:

> Because I have lodgings in their house, therefore I'm about to marry the daughter?!! No mention of love. Oh no, the gossipers have skipped that part! No. I just move into the house and marry! For Heaven's sake! If anything, there has never been a time when I thought less of getting hitched up than I do today! And for what? Money? The last thing I want is a rich wife (in any case the Webers are hardly rich), but even if I could make my fortune by marrying, I should never consider it, for my mind is entirely taken up by very different matters. Has God given me my talent just so I can attach myself to a wife and waste my finest years in idleness? I am only just beginning to live! Mind you, I have nothing against marriage as such, but at this time of my life it would be the greatest folly.

Whether he really believed this, or whether he was simply telling Leopold what he thought he wanted to hear, we shall never know. Five months later, however, the scene had changed to a degree where it was no longer possible to conceal from Leopold that marriage was now very much on his mind. The way he justified this to his ever-anxious father strains credulity:

> Natural urges and desires are as alive in me as in any other man – even more so, perhaps, than in many. But I simply cannot live as most young men of my generation do these days. For a start, I have too much religion; secondly, I have too much love of my neighbour and too deep a sense of honour to seduce an innocent girl; and thirdly, I have too much horror and revulsion, too much dread of diseases and too much concern for my health to fool around with whores. I can swear that I have never had relations of that sort

with any woman. Not one. Besides, if such a thing had happened, I would never have kept it from you; to err, after all, is natural enough in a man, and to err once would be mere weakness... But because of my disposition, which as you know inclines more to a peaceful and homely existence than to revelry, I, who from my boyhood have never been used to looking after my own belongings, linen, clothes, and so on, cannot think of anything more necessary to me – than a wife.

Mozart's generalised thoughts on marriage were prompted by a very specific attachment. In Vienna he felt strongly drawn to Aloysia's younger sister Constanze, whom he took to be the Cinderella of the family. His feelings ripened into love; and before long he asked her to marry him. This, though, was no mere retread of his infatuation with Aloysia. It was no grand passion. There was no feverish euphoria, no obsessive, bittersweet torment. The relationship was happy, warm, comfortable – and filled with sympathetic admiration. But again there was that Mozartian detachment. As he reported to Leopold:

She takes on responsibility for the whole household and yet to judge from their attitudes you would think she did nothing right. Oh, my most beloved father, I could fill page after page with descriptions of what I've seen in that house... She is not ugly, though one could hardly say she is beautiful. Her whole beauty is in two little black eyes and a lovely figure. She has no wit, but sufficient common sense to fulfil her duties as a wife and mother. Far from being extravagant, she is generally shabbily dressed, for what little her mother has managed to do for her children, she has done for the others, but never Constanze. Moreover, she understands housekeeping and has the kindest heart one could ever imagine. I love her and she loves me with all her soul. Tell me if I could possibly wish myself a better wife.

Mozart's wife
Constanze
(1762–1842)

That last simple request, and all it represented, triggered the biggest rift between father and son, from which, despite superficial patchings-up, neither would ever fully recover. After a few bitter exchanges, Leopold, justifiably feeling that he had been superseded in Mozart's life, erected an impenetrable wall of silence. Month after month, his son's letters went unanswered, perhaps even unopened. As the date of the wedding approached, Mozart repeatedly begged his father to give it his blessing:

My dearest, most beloved father, I beseech you again, I implore you, by all you hold dearest in the world, please to grant us your consent to our marriage... My heart is weary with anxiety and aching with sorrow, and my thoughts are all a jumble; in circumstances like these, how can I hope to think and work to any worthwhile purpose? Answer me, please. Answer me. I beg you.

Despite the rhetorical question, Mozart was in fact well able to think and work. Indeed, his new opera, *The Abduction from the Seraglio*, scored the greatest success of his career to date at its opening on 16 July 1782. Now, at last, Leopold broke his silence, but not as Mozart would have liked. In his reply Mozart wrote bitterly:

Your letter of the 26th arrived today. What a cold, uncaring thing, such as I could never have anticipated in response to the news of my opera's great reception. I thought when I sent you the score that you would hardly be able to open the package in your excitement and eagerness to see your son's work, which, far from merely pleasing, is making such a tremendous sensation in Vienna. But no. You... have not had the time!

Still the longed-for consent to the marriage was withheld. Mozart and Constanze married, without it, on 4 August 1782. On the following day, a letter from Leopold arrived, making it plain that Mozart need no longer expect any support from his forsaken father. With a heavy heart, Mozart took up his pen and wrote a brief account of what had been, for him, the most important day of his life:

Well, it's over now. I beg your pardon for my all too hasty trust in your fatherly love. In confessing this, I give you fresh proof of my love for truth and my hatred of a lie. My darling wife will shortly be asking her dearest, most beloved Papa-in-law for his fatherly blessing and her beloved sister-in-law for the continuance of her most valued friendship. The only people who attended the wedding were her mother and her youngest sister, Herr von Thorwart as guardian and witness for both of us, Herr von Cetto, district councillor, who gave away the bride, and Gilowsky who was my best man. When we had been joined together, both my wife and I began to weep. And then all present, even the priest, wept too, at seeing how much our hearts were moved.

Of all the wedding presents the couple could have hoped for, none gave them greater joy, or augured better for their future happiness in Vienna, than the resounding success of *The Abduction from the Seraglio.*

Even without Leopold's blessing, the Mozarts began their married life in a state of unalloyed happiness, conviviality and the justified hope of real prosperity. The greatest hope, of course, now bolstered by ever-increasing support from the aristocracy and his rapturous reception by the Viennese public, was that Mozart would be given an appointment by the Emperor. But the months went by and nothing happened. Mozart began to mutter about moving to Paris (curious, given his failure there before) or even to London. Perhaps to demonstrate that he meant business, he began having regular lessons in English. In all likelihood, much of it was a bluff. In any case, he set about laying the foundations of his new Viennese career, independently of private patronage, placing his main hopes on teaching, the sale of his works, and the revenue from public concerts which he himself would set up. On top of this, he would write music to specific commissions, while his greatest ambitions were rooted, as ever, in the opera house. In quality, quantity and variety, the music that poured from his pen in these early Viennese years is little short of miraculous.

The newly-weds led a lively social life, not skimping on

entertainment, food or drink. From the days of his youth, when the food he most fancied was liver dumplings and sauerkraut, Mozart's culinary tastes had undergone considerable sophistication. Visitors to the couple's apartment might be offered such fare as roast pheasant, a variety of rare meats, oysters, glacé fruits, and a range of fine wines, including Moselle and champagne. In January of 1783, to celebrate the new year and Constanze's first pregnancy, the Mozarts held a ball in their own spacious quarters which lasted from six in the evening till seven the following morning. From the beginning, they tended to live well beyond their means. The lavish gifts from royalty in Mozart's childhood and early teens had left him with expensive tastes. Whatever his financial circumstances, he had an almost compulsive love of the finest clothing (when Clementi first saw him, on the occasion of their pianistic 'duel', he mistook him for a senior chamberlain or a court official). He also developed his own special means of acquiring it. Witness this note to one of his Viennese patrons, the Baroness Waldstätten:

Dearest Baroness,

...About that beautiful red coat, which attracted me so, please, please let me know where it is to be had and how much it costs. I was so enchanted by its splendour that I failed to register its price. I simply have to have one like it, for it will do perfect justice to certain buttons which I have long coveted. I saw them once, while choosing some for a suit. They were in the button factory in the Kohlmarkt. They are mother-of-pearl with a few white stones round the edge and an exquisite yellow stone in the centre. I like all my things to be of good quality, genuine and beautiful. Why is it, I wonder, that people who could never afford it would like to spend a fortune on such articles, and those who can, do not do so?

The ploy paid off, as it usually did. As usual, too, the lady was paid handsomely in the one currency which Mozart always had in abundance:

> *Dearest, Best and Loveliest of All, Gilt, Silvered and Sugared, Most Valued and Honoured Gracious Lady Baroness!*
> *Herewith I have the honour to send your Ladyship, in gratitude for having at once taken so much trouble about the beautiful coat, and for your goodness in finding one just like it, two volumes of plays, a little book of stories – and most particularly, the rondo of which we spoke.*

Unlike those in the Utopian world of his concertos, the tensions in Mozart's life were not easily resolved, least of all, perhaps, with his father. But it was not for want of trying, on either side. On 17 June 1783, Mozart himself became a father, and he too had a son. They named him Raimund Leopold. At the end of the next month, the parents, rather surprisingly, left their first-born with a wet-nurse and set out to visit grandfather Leopold in Salzburg. It was the first time Mozart had seen his father since they had parted in Munich two and a half years earlier, and the first time Constanze had seen him at all. Hopes for a true reconciliation foundered, however, due less to Leopold than to Nannerl, who treated her sister-in-law with undisguised hostility. Her attitude never changed. While they were there, on 19 August, their 'darling, fat, bonny little boy', as Mozart called him, died in Vienna, after only nine weeks of life. It was the first of a series of such bereavements, and it left deep scars.

Interlude V: Mozart in the Theatre

The Operas

Not all Mozart's operas are major works, but by virtue of belonging to the output of the man widely held to be the greatest opera composer in history, all are significant. His first, *Apollo et Hyacinthus,* is significant because it is his first, and because it was written when he was all of eleven. The best known of his childhood operas, the delightful *Bastien und Bastienne,* came a year later, having its premiere at the home of Dr Anton Mesmer. This was followed in 1770 and 1771 respectively by the three-act tragic opera *Mitridate, rè di Ponto* – a major leap forward by any standards, whatever its shortcomings – and *Ascanio in Alba,* both discussed on page 42.

With *Lucio Silla* (1772), another grand three-act opera, we can hear at once what a difference two years made. While still dominated by virtuoso arias in which the singers often seem more important than the characters, there is a marked increase in musical and dramatic atmosphere and real hints of the great Mozart to come.

The first truly great opera is the tragic and passionate *Idomeneo.* By the time he wrote it, Mozart was twenty-four and the prodigy had long since become an absolute, incomparable master. Much of the music is powerfully memorable, the atmosphere and dramatic plotting already anticipate the much later *Don Giovanni*, and the characterisation is vivid, individual and subtle. Electra's aria in Act I is one of the most exciting pieces of musical theatre in the history of opera, terrifying in its fury and intensity; the storm music is a match for anything else in the repertoire; and the psychological insight is almost a match for the intrinsic power of the music. This is the first of Mozart's operas to linger in the mind and heart long after the final curtain has fallen. Apart from the beauty and force of the music, *Idomeneo* marks Mozart's first serious departure from operatic tradition, most notably in his avoidance of decisive endings to most of the arias, creating a musical and dramatic continuity which looks forward to Wagner in the middle of the next century. This was an isolated experiment, however, although he uses similar devices in parts of *Don Giovanni,* and in the finales of *Le nozze di Figaro* ('The Marriage of Figaro'), *Così fan tutte* (literally, 'Thus do all women', but generally given untranslated) and *Die Zauberflöte* ('The Magic Flute').

From here onwards (and not including the two unfinished operas of 1783), Mozart earned his reputation as arguably the greatest opera composer in history with almost every note. The one possible exception to this is his last opera, *La clemenza di Tito* ('The Clemency of Titus', 1791), which is as masterly as ever and contains some very beautiful music, but often seems chilly and formal, with none of the throat-grabbing emotional power of *Idomeneo*. Two years after *Idomeneo* (1780) came *Die Entführung aus dem Serail* ('The Abduction from the Seraglio'), the first of his German operas apart from the youthful *Bastien und Bastienne* and the uncompleted *Zaide* of 1779. This hugely enjoyable and often ravishingly beautiful entertainment is a real one-off: an experiment in mixing various operatic conventions in unconventional ways, combining the dramatic formality of *opera seria* with the comic traditions of *opera buffa* and the spoken dialogue of the classical *Singspiel*. If it does not quite come off theatrically (Mozart had yet to master the concept of serious comedy which reached its high point in *Don Giovanni*), the music alone explains why this remained the most popular of all Mozart's operas during his lifetime.

In the three operas which he wrote with the Italian librettist Lorenzo Da Ponte – *The Marriage of Figaro* (1786), *Don Giovanni* (1787) and *Così fan tutte* (1790) – Mozart reverted to the traditional formulas of Italian comic opera but vastly expanded their scope. Here everything comes together. Comedy and tragedy are now seamlessly integrated, as well as heightened and deepened in psychological insight; the number of

Lorenzo Da Ponte (1749–1838), librettist of Mozart's Marriage of Figaro, Don Giovanni *and* Così fan tutte

ensembles is increased; and the overlong bravura arias of the early Italian operas is nowhere to be found. Everything is in perfect proportion. The characters are subtly differentiated (even within the most complex ensembles), and dramatic pacing and variety of texture are now flawlessly deployed. Each of the operas is a law unto itself, with its own characteristic moods, underlying rhythms and harmonic vocabulary. Nowhere is the integration of opposing extremes more spellbinding than in *Don Giovanni*. Seldom have the dividing lines between good and evil, selfishness and altruism, generosity and malice, bravery and cowardice, truth and deception, or love and lust, proved so disturbingly subtle and fragile. As well as giving the audience a thundering good time, *Don Giovanni* (based on the sexual bravado and warped personality of the infamous Don Juan) is as penetrating a study of human nature as any in the literature, musical or otherwise.

Mozart's last two operas, *La clemenza di Tito* and *The Magic Flute*, were written more or less in tandem but could hardly be more different: the one a formal, almost 'textbook' *opera seria* (a ceremonial commission which he could not afford to turn down), the other a *Singspiel* of unprecedented depth. Compared with the

Italian operas, *The Magic Flute* is simpler in texture, more measured in pace and, except for the Queen of the Night's sensational arias, virtually devoid of bravura. There is a new emphasis on musical declamation, and a sense of allegorical ritual culminating in a dreamlike celebration of Utopian ideals. The opera was greatly influenced by the beliefs, outlook and rites of freemasonry.

Works for Solo Voice and Orchestra

In addition to his operas, Mozart composed some fifty free-standing arias for concert use, the first, K.23, in 1765, when he was nine; the last, K.612, in March 1791. The most famous of these is the remarkable *Ch'io mi scordi di te*, K.505, for soprano, with an elaborate piano obbligato written by Mozart for himself. Several of the concert arias from his Viennese years involve other obbligato instrumental parts, most unusually his last aria, *Per questa bella mano*, K.612, where the bass voice is complemented by a virtuoso part for double bass. In the great soprano aria *Vado, ma dove?*, K.583, the lower woodwind instruments have special prominence. Perhaps the most virtuosic of all (taking the soprano up to a stratospheric top G, one note higher than the Queen of the Night's F) is the much earlier *Popoli di Tessaglia*, K.316. This was written in Mannheim in 1778 for Aloysia Weber, at the time when Mozart was in love with her. From this alone we can deduce that she must have been a very remarkable singer, because, unlike Beethoven, Mozart never wrote beyond the capacities of his intended performers. The most famous of all Mozart's works for solo voice and orchestra, however, is not a mere aria but a three-movement motet, composed near the end of his last journey to Italy, in 1773. *Exsultate, jubilate*, K.165 for soprano, orchestra and organ, represents the highpoint of his early vocal style; and its brilliant concluding 'Alleluia', in particular, has kept it well up in the classical pops for more than 200 years.

Chapter 6

A Friend in Need

A Friend in Need

As his wife remembered many years after his death, Mozart was blessed with an extraordinarily resilient disposition. On their return to Vienna from Salzburg in November 1783, the fount of wonderful music continued undiminished. If work was one bulwark against disappointment, another was Mozart's sense of humour, which right to the end of his life rarely deserted him for long. In the Rondo of his First Horn Concerto, written in 1791 for his friend Joseph Leutgeb, he wrote between the staves of the score, and in several different colours of ink, a bizarre and nonsensical running commentary, supposedly describing a sexual encounter corresponding to events in the music itself:

> *For you, you Ass – Come – quick – get on with it – that's a good lad – Courage! – Are you finished yet? – you beast! – oh what a dissonance! – Oh! – Woe is me!! – Well done, laddie – oh, pain in the balls! – Oh God, so fast! – you make me laugh – help – pause for breath, will you – go on, go on – that's a little better – still not done? – oh you frightful swine! – how charming! – dear one! – little Ass! – ha, ha, ha – take a breath! – But pray do play at least one note, you prick! – Aha! Bravo, bravo, hooray! – You're going to torture me for the fourth time, and thank God it's the last – Oh finish now, oh please! – Oh Damn it! – also bravura? – Bravo! – oh, a bleating sheep – you're finally done? – Oh Thank heavens! – Enough, enough!*

In 1784, the year following their return from Salzburg, Mozart was astonishingly active both as a composer and as a performer. During Lent alone he gave more than seventeen concerts, many by subscription and attended by the cream of Austro-Hungarian society and ambassadors from all over Europe. Vienna's publishers vied with each other to bring out his music, pupils flocked to him, and his income swelled accordingly. In September, the month in which the Mozarts moved to an expensive apartment in one of Vienna's most fashionable districts, their second son, Carl Thomas, was born; in December, Mozart joined the Freemasons, a move which was to have lasting significance in the years ahead. But while Mozart's circle of friends was ever widening, and his social life expanding, his father, in Salzburg, was increasingly isolated. In August, at the age of thirty-three, Nannerl had married a widower with five children and had moved to a town some six hours away. When Leopold visited Vienna in February 1785 to see his son and meet his second grandson, he was travelling unaccompanied for the first time in decades. Almost at once, he was drawn into the whirlwind of activity. He stayed for three months, during which he had the honour of meeting one of Mozart's best and most recent friends, Joseph Haydn, twenty-four years Mozart's senior and widely held to be the world's greatest living composer. This was certainly Mozart's view – but not Haydn's. As Haydn said to Leopold: 'I tell you before God, and as an honest man, that your son is the greatest composer known to me, either personally or by reputation. He has taste, and in addition, the most profound mastery of composition.'

Haydn often came to the Mozarts' house to play quartets with his host, who always preferred to take the viola part, and two other noted composers: Johann Baptist Vanhal and the memorably named Carl Ditters von Dittersdorf. What had made the deepest impression on Haydn, however, was the set of six string quartets which Mozart had dedicated to him – and indeed the dedication itself:

> *To my dear friend Haydn.*
>
> *A father who had determined on sending his sons out into the great world, felt himself obliged to entrust them into the care and guidance of a man who enjoyed the greatest fame, and who happened also to be his best friend. In similar fashion I send these six sons of mine to* my *most renowned and highly valued friend. They are the result of a long and laborious toil; but many friends have encouraged me to believe that this toil will be in some degree rewarded, and that these children may one day be a source of consolation to me. But from this moment I transfer to you all rights over them. I entreat you, however, to look with indulgence on those defects which may have escaped the too partial eye of a father, and in spite of these to continue in your generous friendship towards one who so highly appreciates it.*

Perhaps the most famous single feature of that dedication is Mozart's reference to 'laborious toil'. The general impression was then – as it is now – that Mozart never had to labour over anything; that compositions simply flowed from his brain as though he were simply a medium, a conduit straight from God (unlike Beethoven, who seemed to wrestle and struggle over almost everything). The probable truth is that Mozart had not only a phenomenal memory but an extraordinarily organised mind, and that he did virtually all his composing in his head. Writing it out was no more than printing out a document from a computer. The work had already been done. In fact Constanze, many years after his death, recalled how he used to ask her to come in and chat to him while he was writing out his compositions. Her sister, too, left an interesting account:

He was always good-natured, but even at his most cheerful he was very thoughtful and reflective, looking you straight in the eye, considering his answer to any question you might ask him, yet he always seemed somehow to be working away, deep in thought, at something quite different. And except when he was in conversation, he rarely stood still. Even washing his hands in the morning, he would walk up and down, tapping one foot against the other, with a very concentrated expression.

Pierre-Augustin Caron de Beaumarchais (1732–1799)

The number of great works that Mozart produced in the next few years is astonishing enough in itself. When we remember that this was in addition to his duties as teacher and performer, husband and father, and his very active social life, it seems barely credible. By the mid-1780s, however, the character of his music was changing in ways that would significantly affect his future. Much of it was increasingly difficult to play, thereby discouraging the amateur; there was a darkening and intensification of its character and a new daring in its harmonies. The piano concertos, which had been the staples of his 'academies', confronted his hitherto loyal and enthusiastic audiences with a seriousness and inner turbulence which they found unsettling. The great D minor Concerto (K.466), for instance,

Manuscript extract of Mozart's Marriage of Figaro

can safely be described as the first 'tragic' concerto ever written. To the pleasure-loving Viennese, this was a decidedly unwelcome development: they did not come to concerts to have their withers rung.

In contrast, Mozart's next opera, *The Marriage of Figaro*, premiered on 1 May 1786, was a success almost from the start. This was particularly ironic in view of the fact that it was the most politically explosive thing he ever wrote. The play by Beaumarchais on which it was based was a political satire so dangerous that it had been widely banned. Indeed, many of Mozart's supporters thought he was taking an unnecessarily dangerous risk in tackling it. Fortunately, he had the perfect librettist in the Italian poet Lorenzo Da Ponte, who adapted it with extraordinary cleverness, while Mozart's music proved irresistible. It also carried his reputation far beyond Vienna, as he discovered for himself on an all-expenses-paid trip to Prague.

> *At six o'clock I drove to the so-called Bretfeld ball, where the cream of the beauties of Prague are known to gather. I looked on, with the greatest pleasure, while all these people flew about in unfettered enjoyment to the music of my 'Figaro'. For here they talk about nothing but 'Figaro'. Nothing is played, sung or whistled but 'Figaro'. No opera is drawing like 'Figaro'. Nothing, nothing but 'Figaro'. I must say, this is certainly a tremendous honour for me!*

Better still than the success of *Figaro* was the fact that when Mozart left Prague in February 1787 he had a commission for another opera in his pocket. Prague had taken him to its heart in a way that no other city, even Vienna, had ever quite done.

Prague National Theatre; coloured engraving by L. Penchert

Less happy news followed his return to Vienna, however: Leopold, now long back in Salzburg, had fallen seriously ill. Whatever complicated emotions Mozart may have felt at this turn of events, he wrote a letter to his father which has become famous for its almost priestly simplicity and faith. While it probably does represent his own beliefs, it is in fact a paraphrase of masonic writings, and the thoughts of the philosopher Moses Mendelssohn in particular:

Since death, when we come to contemplate it closely, is the true goal of our earthly life, I have achieved such a close relationship with this truest friend of all humanity that his image, once terrifying to me, has become soothing and consoling! And I thank God for showing me that death is the key to the door of true happiness. I never go to bed at night without reflecting that – young as I am – I may not live to see another day. Yet no-one who knows me could describe me as morbid or melancholy. For this blessing I thank our Creator every day, and profoundly wish that everyone could feel the same.

This was the last contact between father and son. Just over a month later, at the end of May, Leopold died. The only hard evidence we have of Mozart's reaction is a rather cold and businesslike letter to his sister. When his pet starling died a few days later, however, he gave it a fully fledged funeral in his back garden.

Most of 1787 was taken up with the composition of the new opera for Prague, *Don Giovanni*, again to a libretto by Da Ponte. By this time, clouds were beginning to gather. Attendance at Mozart's academies had dropped to the point where he had to abandon them altogether. *Don Giovanni* had a troubled birth (mostly because it proved unexpectedly difficult to sing and to stage) and, though it was a triumph in Prague, it scored only a moderate success in Vienna. Today many musicians and music

Oldest playbill in existence for a performance of Don Giovanni *in Prague, 23 September 1788*

lovers regard it as the greatest opera ever written.

It was a measure of their plummeting income that the Mozarts were now forced to move, for at least part of the year, to the outskirts of Vienna, where the living was cheaper. On the positive side, Mozart was finally granted an official appointment – as Court Chamber Musician, a position that required him to do little more than write dances for the annual court balls at the Emperor's palace. For various reasons, many beyond Mozart's control, the family fell rapidly into debt. The political situation worsened, Austria was drawn into the war between Russia and the Ottoman Empire, much of the male aristocracy left Vienna for the front, and imperial subsidies for the arts quickly fell by the wayside. Theatres were closed; opera companies were disbanded. Through a combination of military action and disease, 170,000 soldiers were immobilised and more than 33,000 died, all within the space of a year. In 1788 rioting broke out on the streets of Vienna, triggered in part by the shortage of bread, but also by political unrest. These events, combined with his chronic tendency to overspend, brought Mozart from high-society celebrity to the status of genteel beggary, a situation exacerbated by the death of a daughter and the serious illness of his wife. Of their four children, only one was still living. Mozart's pathetic begging letters to a wealthy fellow-mason, Michael Puchberg, still make poignant reading:

Great God! I would not wish my present circumstances on my worst enemy. And if you, my most valued friend and brother, forsake me now, then we are truly lost, both my unfortunate and blameless self and my poor sick wife and child. I would never presume to write to you if I weren't certain that you understand my innocence in the terrible plight that has befallen us. And my God! Here I am, coming to you not with thanks alone but with fresh pleas for your help! Instead of repaying what I already owe you, I come begging you for yet more money! If you are my friend, and truly know me, you must recognise the anguish this causes me. But I must mention that in spite of my terrible condition I elected to give subscription concerts at home so that I might at least meet my present expenses, for I was utterly convinced of your friendly assistance. But even this has failed. Unfortunately Fate is so much against me, though only in Vienna, that even when I want to, I can make no money.

The implication of that phrase 'even when I want to' is puzzling. When, in such condition, would he not want to? Puchberg

responded generously, but only a short time later Mozart's spirits
sank still lower:

> I have been living in such unutterable misery, that not only have
> I been unable to go out, for sheer grief, but could not even write.
> My poor dear wife is quite extraordinarily resigned, awaiting
> recovery or death with a truly philosophic calm. But I cannot hold
> back my tears.

Interlude VI: Mozart and Chamber Music

In Mozart's chamber music we have one of the greatest treasuries in music. Between the ages of six and eight he composed, probably with Leopold's help, six sonatas for keyboard and violin. In 1768, aged twelve, he wrote a pair of string duos for the unusual combination of violin and double bass. Within a decade he was already a master of the genre, while from the time of his mid-twenties there are simply no minor works. In chamber music, Mozart's breakthrough to authentic greatness came in Paris in the summer of 1778, with the elegiac, even tragic E minor Violin Sonata, K.304. Like the A minor Piano Sonata, K.310, this was written in the wake of his mother's death; and it is not, perhaps, too far-fetched to see it as a sublimation of his grief.

The most significant difference between chamber and orchestral music is not of size but of kind. Rightly, and delightfully, called 'the music of friends', chamber music – at least for strings – is written primarily for players. The qualification is necessary because wind instruments, with their tonal variety and penetrating sound, were long associated with outdoors entertainment and with banquets, where they provided the dinner music (hence the German term *Tafelmusik* – 'Table Music'). Wind ensembles also had military band associations – hardly conducive to a feeling of intimacy. Most composers of the

Classical era wrote agreeable music for wind band. It was Mozart alone, however, who lifted it into the realm of highest art.

Music for Wind Ensemble

One of the many memorable features of old Austria was the celebration of innumerable occasions by the performance of music in the open air. As early as 1684 we find an English traveller writing from Vienna that a serenade was played before his window almost every evening.

In Mozart's Salzburg there were two kinds of serenade: those for full orchestra enhanced the grandeur of great civic occasions, while the smaller 'divertimentos', generally featuring half a dozen players – usually two oboes, two horns and two bassoons – added to the gaiety of family celebrations (there were no clarinets in Salzburg at that time). Mozart had been writing accomplished and attractive music for winds since 1773, when he was seventeen, but in the early 1780s he composed three epoch-making masterpieces, the last of them unprecedented in both scale and quality. First, in 1781, came the Serenade in E flat, K.375. This occasional piece, composed for itinerant musicians, is not only the most difficult to play of all Mozart's music for wind instruments but the first Classical work for wind ensemble that can safely be described as a masterpiece. It was followed a year later by the equally wonderful though more sombre Serenade in C minor, K.388, which he later transcribed for string quintet. In either guise this is one of the most exalted works in the chamber repertoire and is Mozart's only serenade in the minor mode. Next, however, came a miracle: the almost symphonic Serenade in B flat for 13 Wind Instruments, K.361. Written, or at least completed, in 1784, this seven-movement work of roughly an hour's duration is generally regarded as the greatest work for wind ensemble ever composed. For Mozart the master of instrumental colour, it was a dream come true. In 1778 he first heard the famous Mannheim Orchestra. 'Oh,' he wrote to Leopold back in Salzburg, 'if only we had clarinets too. You have no idea of the glorious effect of a symphony with flutes, oboes and clarinets.' Six years later, in this Serenade, he created a marvel of subtle tone-painting. As well as clarinets, he was able to use two basset-horns (lower-pitched cousins of the clarinet), two pairs of horns in different keys, two oboes, two bassoons and a string double bass. After this extraordinary work, Mozart, with one exception, confined his exploitation of woodwind colour to the orchestra – in his symphonies and, especially, his piano concertos, where the winds serve as celestial mediators between keyboard and strings. The exception is his Quintet in E flat for piano and wind, K.452, which he considered to be the best thing he had composed to date. It has the further distinction of being the first work for this combination ever written. The second, directly modelled on it, was by Beethoven.

Music for String Ensemble

Mozart began writing works for string ensembles when he was eleven. By the time of his first quartet masterpiece, fifteen years later, he had honed his skills on thirteen string quartets and one trio. The principal catalyst for his leap into greatness as a quartet composer seems to have been the appearance of Haydn's Op. 33 quartets in 1782. These were the first quartets in which the four instruments (two violins, viola and cello) conversed together on more-or-less equal terms, and in which form and texture derive equally from the organic development and integration of themes. Haydn's achievement was both an inspiration and a challenge to Mozart, not in the sense of competition but in terms of his own compositional abilities. From the G major Quartet, K.387, dated 31 December 1782, his every work in the medium was a masterpiece

– as acknowledged by Haydn himself, to whom, as we have seen, the first six great quartets were formally dedicated in 1785.

After these, Mozart wrote four more quartets, each adding new subtleties and resources to the craft and understanding of the medium. While the string quartets from 1782 onwards have long since become a prominent part of our musical heritage, two other masterpieces of equal quality remain little known: the string duos for violin and viola, K.423 and 424, which Mozart wrote in 1783 for Michael Haydn (Joseph's brother, in service at Salzburg) to pass off as his own. If the deception worked, then the Archbishop must have been even less musical than Mozart gave him credit for. Apart from anything else, the works are diabolically clever, using the technique of double-stopping (playing two notes at once on a string instrument) and other devices to create the impression that four, not two, instruments are playing. In any case, Michael Haydn could no more have written these than he could have flown to the moon. Another sadly unfamiliar work is the masterly and profound Divertimento in E flat, K.563, for violin, viola and cello, in which Mozart draws textures of astonishing richness and variety from his three instruments.

For many musicians, Mozart's greatest chamber works for strings are the last four of his six quintets for two violins, two violas and cello: K.515 in C, K.516 in G minor (both 1787), K.593 in D (1790) and K.614 in E flat (1791). Texturally, formally, contrapuntally, expressively, these are as innovative and as involving as anything he wrote. They are only marginally harder to listen to than the string quartets, and then only by virtue of having five parts instead of four to follow.

Strings Plus One

Apart from the works with piano, Mozart's most substantial chamber works for strings plus one contrasting instrument are the Oboe Quartet in F, K.370, the Horn Quintet in E flat, K.407, and the dark-hued Clarinet Quintet in A, K.581. The popular flute quartets make for very agreeable listening, but few would classify them as major works.

Piano Plus

In addition to the Quintet for piano and wind, and various negligible childhood works, Mozart wrote two great quartets for piano and strings, K.478 and 493, six piano trios (for the standard combination of piano, violin and cello), and sixteen violin sonatas. In each of these categories, his most important achievement, historically speaking, was to liberate the strings from the purely accompanying role previously assigned to them. Mozart's early violin sonatas were conventionally billed as sonatas 'for piano, with violin accompaniment' – a concept which, despite his example, continued to thrive into the early years of the nineteenth century. But in the sonatas he composed from 1778 onwards violin and piano are absolute equals.

In late-eighteenth-century piano trios (including Haydn's), the cello was given little else to do but reinforce the bass line of the piano part. Mozart's achievement was to emancipate the cello, not only in his later piano trios but also in his two piano quartets. By its very nature the piano is first among equals; but in trios and quartets alike the textures are unprecedentedly democratic. As ever, opera-influenced dialogue is the cornerstone of Mozart's mature style (see Interlude III). The only one of his chamber works to combine three different instrumental families is the Clarinet Trio in E flat, K.498 for piano, clarinet and viola, another darkly coloured, richly lyrical work, allegedly written in a bowling alley or skittles hall.

Chapter 7

The Road to
the Requiem

The Road to the Requiem

In 1788, despite the downward-spiralling change in his fortunes, Mozart wrote two superb piano trios, one of his best known piano sonatas (the 'easy' C major, K.545), most of his last piano concerto, and (among still other things) his last three symphonies. This final symphonic trilogy crowns a series which, along with Haydn's symphonies, had in less than two decades transformed the medium from a lightweight diversion to the highest pinnacle of musical art.

With Viennese commissions now thin on the ground, Mozart decided to revive his long-abandoned career as a travelling virtuoso, in the hope that as well as bringing in much-needed money it might lead to further commissions. He was only partially successful. The reports in his letters to Constanze were depressingly consistent: 'My concerts have succeeded brilliantly in reaping the greatest honour and praise, but have failed utterly where money is concerned.' Just what became of Mozart's money is not at all clear. Certainly he earned some, and just as certainly it did not go to paying off his debts. Whatever his mood, the tour was not without its peaks, among them a very valuable commission, from the King of Prussia, for a group of string quartets. Though not ungenerous, it was hardly enough to turn the tide. It did, though, result in three luminous masterpieces, K.575, 589 and 590. There were improvements, too, on the home front. Back in Vienna, a revival of *The Marriage of Figaro* led to a new operatic commission. The result, *Così fan tutte*, was yet another masterwork, though the supposed immorality of the plot deafened many confirmed Mozartians to the transcendent quality of the music. Indeed, this went on long after Mozart's death, affecting even Wagner, who knew a thing or two about immorality himself: 'Oh how doubly dear and above all honour is Mozart to me, that it was not possible for him to invent music for *Così* like that of *Figaro*! How shamefully that would have desecrated Music!'

One of the most touching and pathetic features of this difficult time is the character of Mozart's letters to his wife, which convey a combination of love, determined optimism and deep discouragement:

Oh my dearest little wife, I positively ache for news of you. I am thoroughly resolved to earn as much money as possible here and then come back to you with a joy that lies beyond description. And what a marvellous life we shall then lead! I shall continue to strive with such unceasing industry that, come what may, we shall never be condemned again to suffer the desperate straits which presently afflict us. Farewell, then, my love, for now. Give my greetings to the few friends who wish me well. Take care of your health, which is more precious to me than you can ever know, and be ever my Constanze as I shall ever be your MOZART.

A short while later he wrote:

A struggle is going on in my heart between my yearning for you and my desire to bring home a lot of money. I've often thought of travelling still further afield, but whenever I do, I'm assailed by thoughts of how bitterly I should regret it if we were to be separated for such an uncertain prospect (and maybe to no purpose

*whatever). Already it feels to me as though I'd left you years ago.
Oh my love, if only you were with me I might decide more easily,
but I love you too much to bear long periods without you. Only
love me half as much as I love you, and I shall be content.*

*P.S. The page above has been watered by my tears. But,
come! I must cheer up – catch! – a swarm of kisses are flying
about! Oh, the very devil! – Here is a whole crowd of them! But Ha!
Ha-Ha!... I've just caught three! – and (m-m-m), they're delicious!*

While there is no doubt over the genuineness of Mozart's
emotions here, there is evidence that all may not have been what
it seemed on this tour. At the beginning, Mozart wrote to
Constanze every two or three days – not a rate which one would
expect him to continue indefinitely, but indicative, like the
content of the letters themselves, of his love and concern for her
(she was pregnant again, and in uncertain health). After his letter
of 16 April, however, the letters cease altogether. A whole month
passes before a distraught Constanze hears from him again, all
her letters to him having gone unanswered. When at last she
hears from him again (he clearly having heard from her), he
carries on for some time as though nothing had happened:

Leipzig, 16 May 1789

Dearest, most beloved little wife of my heart!
*What? I am still in Leipzig? My last letter, dated 8 or 9 May, told
you, it is true, that I was leaving at two o'clock that night; but the
insistent requests of my friends persuaded me not to make the whole
of Leipzig suffer for the shortcomings of one or two people, but to give
a concert on Tuesday the 12th. From the point of view of applause
and glory this concert was absolutely magnificent, but the profits
were wretchedly meagre. Madame Duschek, who happens to be in
Leipzig, sang at it. The Neumanns of Dresden are all here too. The*

pleasure of being as long as possible in the company of these dear good people has up to the present delayed my journey. I wanted to get away yesterday, but could find no horses. I'm having the same difficulty today. For at the present moment everyone is trying to get off, and the number of travellers is simply enormous. But we should be on the road tomorrow at five o'clock.

Only now does he turn to the urgent matter at hand:

My love! I am very sorry (and yet perhaps a little glad) that you are in the same state as I have been. No, no! I would rather that you had never been in the same sad situation and I hope and trust that at the time I am writing this letter, you will at last have received at least one of mine. God knows what the explanation for all this may be! I received in Leipzig on 21 April your letter of 13 April. Then I spent seventeen days in Potsdam without any letters from you. Not until 8 May did I receive yours of 24 April, while apart from this I have not received any, with the exception of one dated 5 May, which came yesterday. For my part, I wrote to you from Leipzig on 22 April, from Potsdam on the 28th, again from Potsdam on 5 May, from Leipzig on the 9th, and now I am writing on the 16th. The strangest thing of all is that we should both have found ourselves in the same sad situation at the same time. I was very anxious from 24 April until 8 May, and to judge from your letter this was also the time when you were worried. I trust that by now you will have got over this. And my consolation is that soon letters will no longer be necessary, for we shall be able to talk to each other and kiss and press each other to our hearts. In my last letter I told you not to write to me any more; and that is the safest course. But I am now asking you to reply to this letter, and to address it to Duschek at Prague. You must put it in a proper envelope and ask him to keep it until my arrival. I shall probably have to spend at least a week in Berlin. So I shall not be able to

reach Vienna before 5 or 6 June – ten or twelve days after you
receive this. One thing more about the loss of our letters. I also
wrote to our dear friend Puchberg on 28 April. Please give him a
thousand greetings from me and thank him on my behalf. A
thousand thanks for the account of Seydelmann's opera.

Farewell, dear little wife. Please do all the things I have
asked you to do in my letters, for what prompted me was love –
real, true love; and love me as much as I do you.
I am ever
Your only true friend and faithful husband, W. A. MOZART

W. A. – as though she might have forgotten. This is a very strange
letter. It strains credulity that all their letters, involving a
sequence of different places, could have gone astray, let alone at
exactly the same time. For a start, the postal service was famously
efficient. There is something odd, too, in his manner of citing
chapter and verse where his own letters are concerned. And what
of Madame Duschek, 'who happens to be in Leipzig'? Gossip was
already beginning to circulate about her friendship with Mozart.
When all the evidence is laid out, the suspicion is strengthened
that they were more than merely friends. Also plain from
Mozart's letters is the fact that Constanze nursed chronic doubts
about her husband's fidelity – doubts which he was naturally at
pains to allay.

In letter after letter he describes the solitary life he is leading,
almost as though it were on her behalf: 'Please remember that
every night before going to bed I talk to your portrait for a good
half hour and do the same each day when I awake...' In one
notable case he assures her not only of his love but also of his
pent-up lust:

I intend to sleep... on the 4th — the 4th ! – with my darling little
wife. Arrange your dear sweet nest very daintily – for my little

*fellow richly deserves it! He has been behaving himself very well
and is only longing to possess your sweetest [word obliterated]. Just
picture that scallywag to yourself! As I write he rises to the table
and looks at me, questioningly. I box his ears properly – but the
rogue is simply [word obliterated] and now the wretch burns only
more fiercely, indeed can hardly be restrained... Oh, how glad
shall I be to be with you again, my darling! But the first thing I
shall do is to take you by your front curls; for how on earth could
you think, or even imagine, that I had forgotten you? How could I
possibly do so? For even imagining such a thing, however, you will
get on the very first night a thorough spanking on your dear little
kissable arse. You may count on this!*

In spite of the downturn in their fortunes, Mozart returned to
Constanze and Vienna full of energy and an almost mischievous,
devil-may-care impulse to explore new paths in music. This
hardly seemed a safe proposition. But it paid off brilliantly,
nowhere more so than in *Così fan tutte*, which had its first
performance one day before Mozart's thirty-fourth birthday.

Così was very much a connoisseur's opera, not least in its
emphasis on ensembles rather than dazzling solo arias. The
extent of its success was surprising even to Mozart. Even at this
low point of his professional life he refused to take the easy route
and write mainly 'popular' works for mass consumption.
Whatever his worldly problems, his genius was at its height. He
knew it, and he felt an almost holy obligation to follow wherever
it led him. Even though he was reduced to accepting commissions
for freak instruments like mechanical organs and the weird,
otherworldly glass harmonica, he wrote masterpieces for them
out of all proportion to their limited capacity to do them justice.

With the death of one emperor and the accession of another
in 1790, Mozart's hopes first rose and then plummeted. An
important position once again eluded him, and his health went

into decline. In the late summer he began to suffer from headaches and generalised pain, making it difficult for him to sleep; and on Constanze's next visit to Baden to take the waters, Mozart went with her. In the autumn he undertook another tour, to Frankfurt, which proved to be as fruitless as the last. On the way back to Vienna he notably failed to take the opportunity to visit his sister when he passed near her home. More puzzlingly, he chose to pass up another opportunity when he got back home. The manager of the King's Theatre in London invited him to come to England for six months and write two operas for a fee of £300 each, a colossal sum in those days. It was the offer of a lifetime; and for reasons which have never been fully explained, Mozart turned it down. Constanze's precarious health may have been a factor, though he makes no mention of this in his letters. By contrast, Haydn had accepted an invitation to London after the death of Prince Nicolaus Esterházy. On the eve of his departure in December 1790, Mozart dined with him, and was uncharacteristically emotional. He seemed agitated, obsessed by the conviction that he would never see Haydn again. How much, if anything, Constanze knew of this remains unknown. It seems improbable that Mozart concealed it from her, but yet more improbable that she would have suppressed it throughout the fifty-two years of life that remained to her.

Haydn departed on schedule, and by the summer of 1791 Mozart was occupied with a new opera, *The Magic Flute* – not this time a royal or even an aristocratic commission, but a theatrical entertainment aimed at the general music-loving public rather than the connoisseur. This is not to say that Mozart was in any sense 'dumbing down'. In *The Magic Flute* he achieves new heights of simplicity; but it is the ultimate simplicity of genius. That said, the work also contains some of the most virtuosic music he ever wrote, most famously the Queen of the Night's fearsome 'vengeance' aria.

Hardly had he finished *The Magic Flute* than he set to work on another, very different masterpiece: the Clarinet Concerto in A. Then, in October, straight after completing the concerto, Mozart embarked on the Requiem that was to prove his final work. It had been anonymously commissioned by a nobleman, one Count Walsegg, who was in the habit of ordering works from distinguished composers, buying exclusive rights, copying them out himself and passing them off as his own. In this case he wanted to commemorate the recent death of his young wife. While at work on the Requiem Mozart fell seriously ill and, according to Constanze, became convinced that he was writing it for himself. He also developed the paranoid fantasy that he had been poisoned. More than two centuries after his death, and despite a host of theories, books, theatrical pieces, television *Mozart on his* programmes and movies, not a shred of evidence has yet been *deathbed during* found to support the claim. Whatever the cause, it became clear *the singing of his* that Mozart might well not live to complete the work. In the last *Requiem*

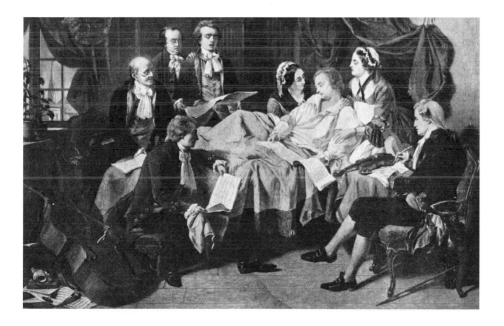

two or three weeks of his life he began giving instructions to his pupil Süssmayr as to how it should be finished.

The account of his last hours is best left to his sister-in-law, Constanze's youngest sister, Sophie, who was with him:

I had just lit the lamp in our kitchen and made some coffee for my mother. I stared into the brightly burning flame and thought to myself, 'I wonder how dear Mozart is.' And at that very moment, the flame went out, as completely as if it had never been lit. But there was no hint of a draught. All of a sudden the most terrible feeling overcame me. I ran as fast as I could to their house. My sister, who was almost despairing, admitted me, saying: 'Oh dear Sophie, thank God you have come. He was so bad last night that I thought surely he was lost. Do stay with me today, for if he has another attack he will die tonight, I know it. Now go and see him.' Trying to contain myself, I went to his bedside. He looked up at me, saying, 'Dear Sophie, how happy I am that you've come. Stay here tonight and see me die.' I tried to control my feelings and persuade him otherwise. But he only replied: 'The taste of death is now on my tongue, and I can already smell the grave. If you don't stay, who will support my dearest Constanze when I am departed?' 'Yes, yes, dear Mozart,' I assured him. Oh God, how I felt! My poor sister beckoned me and entreated me to seek out the priests at St Peter's and implore one of them to come with all speed. I did so; but to begin with they declined and I had great trouble persuading anyone to go to him. I then ran as fast as I could back to my distracted sister. Süssmayr was now at Mozart's bedside. The score of the Requiem was spread out on the quilt and Mozart was explaining to him how he ought to finish it when he was gone. Further, he enjoined his wife to keep his death a secret until she had told Albrechtsberger, who would take charge of the services. After a long search, Dr Closset arrived and ordered cold poultices to be placed on Mozart's burning head, which, however, affected him to such an extent that he fainted, and remained unconscious until he died. His last act was an attempt to express with his mouth the drum passages in the Requiem. I shall never forget that sound. Nor can I describe how his devoted wife in utter misery threw herself on her knees and beseeched the Almighty for His aid. She could not tear herself away from Mozart, no matter how much I begged. If it was possible to aggravate her grief, this was done on the following day, when crowds of people walked past his lifeless body and wept and wailed for him. And do you know, in all my life I never once saw Mozart in a temper, still less, angry.

So said many, though emphatically not the Archbishop of Salzburg. Two days later, Mozart's body was conveyed, unaccompanied, from St Stephen's Cathedral, where his funeral was held, to St Marx's cemetery, some three miles distant. Here it was deposited, in a linen sack, in a mass grave whose exact location has never been found. It should be noted, however, that the circumstances of Mozart's burial were quite common at the time, and not, as one generally hears, an indictment of society's shameful neglect. The Emperor Joseph II had disliked the unnecessary expense of traditional funerals; and under his reign 'sack burials', as they were known, became the norm, as did the custom of the unaccompanied hearse. We should remember, too, that Mozart died with substantial debts, of which the greatest, significantly, were to the tailor, the apothecary and the decorator. There is hardly a description of Mozart's appearance that fails to mention his elegant and fashionable clothing.

If he pondered the fate of his music in posterity, he left no evidence of the fact. It seems unlikely, though, that he would be surprised that his music has long since taken its place at the centre of western musical culture. More than that, it lives on in the hearts of music lovers all over the world.

Interlude VII: The Choral Music

Mozart's religious choral music is often, frankly, disappointing. Although they span the bulk of his composing career, from the Kyrie in F, K.33 to the Requiem, K.626, his sacred works show nothing like the creative journey undertaken in the realms of instrumental and operatic music. Only the most fanatical of his admirers would claim that they give us, on the whole, anything like the best of Mozart. There are exceptions, of course, but not many; and of these, the two greatest – the Mass in C minor, K.427, and the Requiem – were never finished.

The earliest of his sacred works, the aforementioned Kyrie in F, was composed during his visit to Paris in 1766. Next came the *Missa solemnis* in C minor, K.139 (47a), composed for Vienna, where the twelve-year-old Mozart directed its first performance. This was a grand work, with the full panoply of soloists and choir, accompanied by an orchestra of two oboes, four trumpets, three trombones, timpani, strings and organ. Still grander was the Mass in C (the 'Dominicus' Mass), K.66 of 1769, written for Salzburg. It was the last of its kind. With the accession of the Prince-Archbishop Hieronymus Colloredo in 1771 came a new (and to Mozart, unwelcome) austerity. For the duration of his reign, Colloredo decreed that the celebration of the mass should last no more than three quarters of an hour, thus limiting Mozart's contribution to little more than twenty minutes.

As in Mozart's operas, musical considerations often took precedence over word settings, to the annoyance of the Archbishop who favoured precisely the opposite emphasis. Colloredo's austerity alone accounts for the predominance in Mozart's Salzburg masses of short, uncomplicated and chorally declamatory settings, with little or no repetition of phrases. Though none is without its points of interest, it is hard to avoid the sense that they were written to some extent under duress. There were exceptions, of course. The *Missa brevis* in C, K.262, for instance, makes welcome use of the so-called 'recapitulation convention', in which the music of the opening Kyrie returns in the closing Agnus Dei. The best of all, by common consent, is the Mass in C, K.317 (the 'Coronation' Mass). Here we get the recapitulation convention in triplicate: the Agnus Dei again repeats the music of the Kyrie, and both the Gloria and Credo end with the recapitulation of their opening sections. If we add to this Mozart's cavalier treatment of the words   always, of course, to strictly musical ends – we have the makings of a time bomb in Mozart's relations with his employer. Never was an incendiary device more sweetly capped than with the beautiful Agnus Dei. Its ravishing soprano solo (a harbinger of the Countess's 'Dove sono' in *The Marriage of Figaro*) leads to a plea for peace from the four soloists, who are soon joined by the chorus and full orchestra.

The florid, operatic character of that Agnus Dei is a reminder that Mozart's conception of liturgical music was fundamentally influenced by his exposure to Italian traditions on his three extended trips there between 1769 and 1773. Indeed, the Italianate influence on his music in general was very great. When Colloredo, not long after the premiere of the 'Coronation' Mass, demanded that church music should be less elaborate and advocated the introduction of German hymns into the liturgy, the writing was on the wall. It was only a little over a year later that Mozart resigned acrimoniously from the Archbishop's service.

In Vienna, the atmosphere was hardly more conducive to church music than in Salzburg. In the ten years left to him, he wrote only two more masses, neither of which he completed. The first was the towering Mass in C minor, K.427, composed as a hymn of thanksgiving for his marriage to Constanze. Although incomplete, a version of the work (probably just the Kyrie and Gloria) was performed in Salzburg to mark her introduction to Leopold, Nannerl, and the town of his birth. The florid, 'operatic' 'Et incarnatus est' may have been intended for Constanze herself. Notable for its wonderful dialogue with the wind instruments, this has long since found a place of its own in the soprano concert repertoire.

Masses, however, formed only a part of the church music that Mozart wrote for Salzburg. There were offertories, antiphons, motets, a Te Deum, various isolated movements, and, most importantly, four litanies and two sets of vespers. The third and fourth of the litanies – the *Litaniae lauretanae*, K.195 and the *Litaniae de venerabili altaris sacramento*, K.243 – are on a grander scale and more musically interesting than anything prior to the C minor Mass. For many Mozartians, K.243 is the finest of all the Salzburg church works. Richly scored for pairs of flutes, oboes, bassoons, horns, three trombones and strings, four vocal soloists and full chorus, it lasts for roughly forty minutes and holds the attention for most of them, an exception being the showy and over-long tenor solo 'Panis vivus'. Of the two sets of vespers, the second, *Vesperae solennes de confessore* K.339, has proved perennially popular with choirs and music lovers. Nowhere here does one sense the constraints of Colloredo's Salzburg, and the range of styles is virtuosic in its own right. The beautiful soprano aria 'Laudate Dominum', like the Agnus Dei of the 'Coronation' Mass and the 'Et incarnatus est' from the C minor, has escaped to lead an independent life.

Mozart's two famous motets frame most of his career as a

composer of sacred music and could hardly be more different. Of these, the early, operatically flamboyant *Exsultate, jubilate*, K.165 has been mentioned (see page 118). The brief, choral *Ave verum corpus*, K.618 was one of his last completed works. Its unearthly beauty and piercingly affecting harmonies have made it a favourite among music lovers for two centuries, and a staple in the repertories of choirs and choral societies the world over. It was also famously arranged by Tchaikovsky (from Liszt's transcription rather than the original) for his Fourth Orchestral Suite *Mozartiana*.

The story of Mozart's final work, the Requiem, is almost as famous as the work itself. Despite being established over two centuries as one of his most popular works, only the first two movements (and their repetitions much later in the work) are entirely his. Of the rest, Mozart completed about half the movements in vocal score. These were orchestrated by his friend and pupil Franz Xaver Süssmayr, who composed the Sanctus, Benedictus and Agnus Dei entirely by himself – or so he claimed. Given the mediocrity of his own church music, this would indeed have been miraculous. How far he worked on sketches or ideas which Mozart may have played to him on the piano is something we shall never know. What we do know is that, after Mozart's death, Constanze entrusted the score to another of Mozart's pupils, Joseph Eybler, who orchestrated parts of Mozart's manuscript (Eybler, indeed, had been Constanze's first choice to complete the Requiem). Yet a third composer, one Franz Jakob Freystädtler, was also involved at some stage. Just who did what, where and when is unlikely ever to be settled.

Chapter 8

Mozart the Immortal

Mozart the Immortal

With the decline of his fortunes towards the end of his life, Mozart was not merely a casualty of history. He was the prisoner of a creative urge that would not allow him to stand still, both figuratively and literally. Remember his sister-in-law: 'Except when he was in conversation, he rarely stood still. Even washing his hands in the morning, he would walk up and down, tapping one foot against the other, with a very concentrated expression.' We have further testimony from his brother-in-law, the court actor Josef Lange:

> *Never was Mozart less to be apprehended in his speech and action*
> *as a great man than when he was busy with an important work.*
> *Then he spoke not only with haphazard confusion, but sometimes*
> *made jokes of a kind which with him one was not used to; indeed,*
> *he even deliberately neglected his behaviour...*

The writer Karoline Pichler paints a more specific and more disconcerting picture when she describes him at such moments 'leaping over tables and chairs, miaowing like a cat and turning somersaults like an unruly boy'. Evidence of this kind has led to suggestions that Mozart suffered from Tourette's Syndrome. This would seem to be strengthened by his propensity to scatological humour and verbal obscenity. Ultimately, however, such theories are interesting but irrelevant. All that matters is the music. And the music, more or less from 1785 onwards, shows Mozart embarking on a new voyage of experiment and discovery. Three developments in particular caused problems for some of his listeners: firstly, his expansion of the orchestra in his operas to a symphonic richness and density (*Figaro, Don Giovanni*); secondly, an increased use of dissonant and chromatic harmonies (*Don Giovanni*, the 'Haydn' Quartets, the B minor *Adagio*, A minor Rondo and Minuet in D for piano); and thirdly, his Shakespearean mixture of tragedy and comedy (*Don Giovanni* again). These three interrelated developments were profoundly influential, not least on Haydn, whose 'Representation of Chaos' at the start of his oratorio *The Creation* would arguably never have been written but for the slow introduction to the C major Quartet which Mozart dedicated to him. Indeed, one could draw a straight line from Mozart's late works to the epoch-making harmonics of Wagner's *Tristan und Isolde* three quarters of a century later.

Together and singly, all these new directions expanded the range of dramatic, emotional and spiritual expression. In *Figaro* and *Don Giovanni*, the orchestra is on a par with the singers – anticipating, developing and unifying the musical events unfolding on the stage. The increased use of dissonant chromaticism added rich new colours to music's expressive palette, both tonal and psychological, and anticipated the dominance of inner turbulence that was central to Romanticism. Likewise, Mozart's unique mingling of tragedy and comedy deepened the dramatic and psychological power of ambiguity and its potential for suspense. In this, Mozart's later music was both revolutionary and prophetic.

By the time of his death, Mozart was acknowledged as a controversial as well as a great composer. Munich's *Allgemeine musikalische Zeitung* warned its readers to be wary of music in which 'one audacious transition closely follows upon another'. Almost twenty years after Mozart's death, the critic J.B. Schaul characterised his harmonies as 'hard and sophisticated', leading listeners 'between steep rocks into a thorny forest in which flowers grow but thinly'. In the year of Mozart's death, another critic wrote of his 'most peculiar traits', citing his 'bizarre flights of the soul' and his 'indulgence in the strangest paradoxical turns'. As late as 1826, only a year before the death of Beethoven, the Swiss composer Hans Georg Nägeli complained of the exaggerated, debauching contrasts in Mozart's music. Mozart's expansion of the opera orchestra was only slightly less contentious than his harmonies. After a performance of *The Marriage of Figaro* the Emperor Joseph II, no less, allegedly complained that Mozart had 'completely blanketed the singers with his full orchestra'. In the *Journal des Luxus und der Moden* of 1791 we read that Mozart's operatic orchestra is 'artificial, weighty, and overloaded with instruments'.

In contemporary criticisms of Mozart, the charge that his music is 'overloaded' and 'overstuffed' was chanted almost like a mantra. Another (this time highly ironic) criticism was also levelled at him, even by some of his self-confessed admirers. Thus we find the composer-conductor Bernhard Anselm Weber observing that 'the wealth of beautiful detail almost crushes the soul'. The same point made was made Dittersdorf:

> *I have never yet found anyone who possessed such an astonishing wealth of ideas. I only wish he were not so lavish with them. He leaves his hearers out of breath, for scarcely has one thought arrived than another stands already in its place, thus driving out the first, and this goes on continuously without cease, so that in the end none of these real beauties can be preserved in the memory.*

A virtually identical criticism was articulated by Adolph von Knigge eleven years earlier in response to hearing *The Abduction from the Seraglio*: 'One beautiful thought drives out another, thus removing it from the admiration of the hearer.'

Again and again the same point is made: that Mozart's music, now so often identified with simplicity, is difficult to listen to, fit only for connoisseurs. Thus Ernst Ludwig Gerber in his *Historisch-Biographisches Lexicon der Tonkünstler* in 1790: 'This great master has from his early acquaintance with harmony become so deeply and inwardly intimate with it, that it is hard for an unskilled ear to follow his works. Even the skilled must hear his things several times.' Among these was the poet Goethe:

> *Recently* Die Entführung aus dem Serail *by Mozart was given. Everyone professed themselves for the music. The first time they played it quite moderately; the text itself is very bad, and I also was not at one with the music. The second time it was very badly played, and I even left. Yet the piece maintained itself and everyone praised the music. When they gave it for the fifth time, I went to it again. They acted and sang better than before, I separated out the text and now understand the difference between my initial judgement and the impression on the public. I now know where I am.*

Ironically for a composer whose first requirement of music and its performance was that it should exhibit 'taste and feeling', Mozart was roundly attacked for his lack of both. After the first Berlin performance of *Don Giovanni*, a local critic thundered, 'In this opera the eye was satiated, reason grieved, morality offended, and virtue and feeling trampled upon by vice.' 'Oh!' cried another to Mozart in the *Chronik von Berlin*, 'had you not so greatly wasted the power of your mind! Had your feeling been more in correspondence with your fancy!' The *Musikalisches Wochenblatt* printed a letter from an irate reader who proclaimed, 'I never heard a single profound expert praise him [Mozart] as a correct, much less a perfect composer. Least of all will the *tasteful* critic believe him to be a composer who is correct in regard to poetry, or even sensitive.' In 1801 we find the Parisian correspondent of the *Allgemeine musikalische Zeitung* lamenting that 'Mozart possesses more genius than taste'. And later, on *The Magic Flute*: 'In this opera clowns and sages, together with animals and all the other elements, form a chaos, in order (as I suppose) to make the miraculous in the serious part of the opera comprehensible, and to make war on good taste and sane reason in a spectacle that dishonours the poetry of our age.' On *Don Giovanni*, the *Chronik von Berlin* outdid itself:

> *Music for the theatre knows no other rule, and no other judge, than the heart... What the composer must express is not an overloaded orchestra, but heart, feeling, and passion. Only as he writes in a great style, only then will his name be given to posterity. Grétry, Monsigny, and Philidor prove this [!]. Mozart, in his* Don Giovanni, *intended to write something uncommonly, inimitably great. There is no doubt the uncommon is here, but not the inimitably great! Whim, caprice, ambition, but not heart, created* Don Giovanni.

In 1793, a mere two years after the composer's death, a critic for the *Allgemeine musikalische Zeitung* grants that 'Mozart was a great genius, but he had no real taste, and little or perhaps no *cultivated* taste. He missed, of course, any effect in his original operas.' Of course! And he goes on, challenging anyone 'to prove that Mozart understood how to treat a libretto correctly'.

It would be wrong to suggest that these attacks on Mozart's music were the norm at any time. They represent a minority view, but they are a significant minority. And many of them may have been provoked by an almost sycophantic enthusiasm. Typical of many such outpourings is the following, from a correspondent in the *Chronik von Berlin* in October 1790:

Mozart belongs among those extraordinary men, whose glory will endure for centuries. His great genius embraces as it were the entire compass of musical art; it is rich in ideas; his works are a torrent, in full flood, which carries forth all in its wake. None before has surpassed him, and deep reverence and admiration will posterity not deny him. One must be still more than a connoisseur to be able to form an opinion of him. What a masterpiece, this music of today! For the connoisseur how interesting! How great, how overwhelming, how enchanting the harmony! But for the great masses too? That is another question.

Thus is Mozart co-opted into the armoury of snobbery.

For all the critical remarks quoted above, there can be no doubt that Mozart's reputation at the time of his death, and in the following decade, stood very high. He was regularly ranked with the more accessible Haydn (and no praise could have been higher). In addition to his greatness as a musician, 'Papa' Haydn was the most *beloved* composer in history, especially in Austria, but also in England and Germany. In the realm of opera, however, Mozart was commonly held to be supreme. Of Haydn's many operas, very few were accorded more than one production. Throughout the 1790s, and into the 1800s, Mozart's operas were widely performed, and repeatedly published. Interestingly, the front-runners were *The Magic Flute* and *Don Giovanni* – the two most contentious – closely followed by *La clemenza di Tito*, thereafter the most neglected of his mature operas.

His major works, relatively few of which were printed in his lifetime, began to appear with increasing frequency, and by 1798, only seven years after his death, two important publishers, Spehr of Brunswick and Breitkopf & Härtel of Leipzig (still going strong at the time of writing) had embarked on collected editions, the former of his keyboard works, the latter more wide-ranging. Several other sets with similar aims were inaugurated in the subsequent decades. Other prominent publishers included the André firm in Offenbach, who collaborated directly with Constanze over much of Mozart's manuscript material and published a lot of it, some in responsible critical editions – a rarity until well into the nineteenth century.

A biography, albeit a brief one, appeared as early as 1793: the belated *Obituary* by Friedrich Schlichtegroll, heavily influenced by the partisan recollections of Mozart's sister. The first important biography, by Franz Niemetschek, followed in 1798. Notable publications in the early part of the nineteenth century included comparisons of Mozart and Haydn by I.F. Arnold (1810) and Stendhal (1814); then, in 1828, Constanze's second husband Georg Nikolaus Nissen produced the most substantial biography to date.

By that time, music, and society, had undergone dramatic changes. Beethoven, Weber and Schubert were dead. Mendelssohn (born 1809), Chopin (1810) and Liszt (1811) were all making international reputations; Schumann (1810) was about to. The Romantic movement was in full swing, bringing with it an unprecedented interest in the past. More of Mozart's music was known to the Romantics than was ever known in his own century, yet most of it still awaited discovery. Even many of the works known to musicians were seldom performed in concert. Mozart's life, as it was handed down, was a gift to the Romantic imagination: the Christ-like child of divine attainments, his rejection by the lords of the earth, his alleged licentiousness, the rift with his father, his fashionable pallor, the 'ghostly' commission of the Requiem by a mysterious stranger clad in grey, his early death (much prophesied in youth), its 'macabre' circumstance (the fabled poisoning – a symbolic crucifixion?), the pauper's burial, the unknown grave, the celestial purity of his music, the shifting balances of good and evil (*Don Giovanni*), the duality of his personality... it made a heady brew. The fact is, however, that it was based, for most non-musicians, on a tiny portion of Mozart's output. The key works, those that gripped the Romantic imagination, were the darker-hued masterpieces: *Don Giovanni*, the G minor Symphony (No. 40), the D minor and C minor Piano Concertos (Nos 20 and 24). At the same time, there was a tendency to romanticise the opposite extreme, to cast Mozart in the role of the delicate and charming angel, the master of decorum and grace, the apogee of 'taste' (this last would have pleased him).

The 'Romantic movement' is a convenient but misleading term. There was nothing monolithic about it. It housed a great diversity of tastes, attitudes and aspirations. At one extreme – to consider only the most prominent composers – were Chopin and Mendelssohn, the most classically minded of the Romantics, both devoted to Mozart and Bach. At the other were the gigantists Berlioz and, one rung down, Meyerbeer. In the middle there was Schumann – an arch-Romantic, an addict of the dual-personality cult as celebrated, indeed largely invented, by the writers Jean Paul and E.T.A. Hoffmann. His view of Mozart compares interestingly with that of Berlioz. First, Schumann:

Clarity, repose, grace, the distinguishing mark of the artworks of antiquity, are also those of the Mozartian school... Should this brilliant manner of thinking and composing perhaps one day be supplanted by a formless mystic one, as it will in time, so may that other ancient art, in which Mozart reigned, not become forgotten.

Elsewhere, scoffing at the poet and aesthetician Schubart's association of certain feelings with particular keys, Schumann writes, 'In G minor he [Schubart] finds discontent, discomfort, worrying anxiety, ill-tempered champing at the bit. Now compare this with Mozart's Symphony in G minor [No. 40] – that floating Grecian grace!'

The interesting point here is that Schubart's characterisations, if we delete 'ill-tempered', are precisely those which most people, then and now, have found in the G minor Symphony. The Romantic Schumann, he of the anguished soul and troubled mind, finds in Mozart a never-never land of repose, 'floating grace' and perfect order. Surprisingly, given the source, this suggests a curious superficiality. But it was hardly an aberration confined to Schumann. It was a commonplace of the time.

But now Berlioz:

> *Mozart, whose operas are all alike in their chill beauty, so trying to the patience!... As for Cimarosa, to the devil with his eternal and unique 'Secret Marriage' which is even more tedious than 'The Marriage of Figaro', without being anywhere near as musical...*

Chill beauty? At least he grants the beauty. But 'tedious'? And why drag in Cimarosa? Truth to tell, there was no dragging needed: Nissen, in his biography, refers to the widespread public ranking of Cimarosa's *Il matrimonio segreto* ('The Secret Marriage') alongside not only *Figaro* but Mozart's comedies in general. Indeed the great Goethe, who had to work at appreciating Mozart, actually preferred Cimarosa.

To put Cimarosa on a par with Mozart is like putting Agatha Christie on a par with Tolstoy. (But then Tolstoy said Beethoven had no talent, so perhaps we should be wary of great writers' musical pronouncements.) Each era sees art through the lenses of its time. Next to the extravagant dramatics of the nineteenth century – from Beethoven to Berlioz, to Liszt and Wagner, to Tchaikovsky, Mahler and Richard Strauss – is Schumann's view to be wondered at? In the context of that century, the 'Dresden China' Mozart that prevailed was a necessary corrective, a refuge, a haven of tranquillity and order in a century of revolution, turmoil and bloodshed. As the century neared its end, Johannes Brahms, whose love and knowledge of Mozart were unexcelled by anyone, looked back with a dispassion that was almost serene:

I understand very well that the new personality of Beethoven, the new outlook, that people accorded his work, let it appear to them greater, more important. But surely fifty years afterwards one must be able to rectify this judgement. I grant you that the Beethoven Concerto [in C minor] is more modern [than Mozart's in the same key], but not as important! I see as well that Beethoven's First Symphony made such a colossal impression on people. That is just the new outlook! But the three last Mozart symphonies are still far more important! Here and there, people are already beginning to sense this!

Whatever the prevailing vision of his music in this time or that, Mozart has been a key factor in the measurement and direction of musical practice from his own time to the present. His influence has been a shaping force in the development of composers as diverse as Beethoven, Schubert, Schumann, Chopin, Mendelssohn, Liszt, Wagner, Bruckner, Mahler, Tchaikovsky, Richard Strauss, Reger, Ravel, Debussy, Stravinsky, Busoni and Schoenberg. This is not the place to cite chapter and verse, which would open the floodgates of compositional jargon; but the influence is analytically demonstrable in the work of every composer mentioned, and probably many more. Nor has his influence been confined to music. He has exercised the minds and engaged the hearts of writers and philosophers including E.T.A. Hoffmann (who exchanged his given third name, Wilhelm, for Amadeus, hence the 'A'), Pushkin, Kierkegaard, Mörike, George Bernard Shaw, Brigid Brophy and many others. His music has also been shown to aid concentration, improve the memory, stimulate thought, enhance imagination, and alleviate depression and anxiety, in countless students, writers, artists and workers, many of whom may never have heard his music before. Not bad going for an eternal child.

The Eighteenth-Century Background

Overview

The eighteenth century has rightly been called 'the century of revolutions' (though the nineteenth can lay equal claim to the title), but the most lasting of these were agricultural, industrial and scientific, not military or political. Human knowledge expanded to an unprecedented degree, with effects on daily life which would eventually eclipse the transient decisions of governments and rulers. Wars, as ever, proliferated, with five in particular having the most lasting impact: the Wars of the Spanish and Austrian Succession, the Seven Years War, and the American and French Revolutions. Despite the gathering groundswell of democracy, absolute monarchies continued to flourish in most parts of the world. Prussia and Russia (the latter, ironically, under the Prussian-born Catherine the Great) became world powers; French power diminished under the increasingly inept rule of Louis XV and Louis XVI; the British Empire expanded, most dramatically in India; and America became a major player on the international political stage. More important, however, than any armed insurrection or expansionist military campaign was the emergence of an increasingly powerful and independent middle class. More than any previous century, the eighteenth was a century of commerce.

World trade was an immediate beneficiary of the

improvements in transport and communications which flowed from the scientific and technological advances then taking place on almost every front. By the mid-century, raw materials were being imported from countries all over the world, often to the social and economic disadvantage of the exporting nations. Europe, on the other hand, profited hugely, exporting a wide range of goods and spawning a large quantity of financial institutions – banks, stock exchanges, insurance companies, and so on. Cheques were increasingly used in place of cash, and the proliferation of paper money increased the amounts that a pedestrian could easily carry. For the newly well-to-do, shopping became a pastime as well as a business.

Among many significant medical advances which substantially improved the quality of life, the most important was the discovery of a vaccine against smallpox – but not before one epidemic in 1719 killed 14,000 people in Paris alone. An unforeseen side-effect of middle-class affluence and improved standards of public and personal hygiene was an increase in population which threatened to outstrip the food supply. Although many did indeed starve, the era saw greater changes in agricultural methods than had occurred for many centuries. Farming became a major industry as the demand for food and wool increased.

Of all eighteenth-century revolutions, though, none had more far-reaching consequences than the Industrial Revolution. Originating in Britain in the middle third of the century, it owed its initial impetus to the invention of the steam engine, first used as a means of draining mines but rapidly put to use in factories. With the unprecedented proliferation of new machinery which vastly increased the speed and output of manufacturing, England became known as 'the workshop of the world', and prospered accordingly. The revolution soon spread to other countries, shifting the balance of power from the aristocratic landowner to the industrial capitalist and creating a large urban (and increasingly vocal) working class.

Yet despite a burgeoning, increasingly prosperous middle class, which made much of 'good manners' and the trappings of gentility, the great majority of the population, in Europe as elsewhere, continued to live in poverty and die early from disease and starvation. Education for the poor was minimal, illiteracy and crime were rife, child labour commonplace and political representation generally non-existent. In the Old World and the New, slavery continued unchecked, although an increasing number of Europeans, particularly in Britain, found the practice repugnant.

In Europe and other parts of the world, the traditional ruling classes came increasingly under threat. Of the numerous insurrections which erupted in the eighteenth century, the first of world significance was the American Revolution (1776–83). From it emerged the newly independent United States, a country of vast resources, whose political creed, resoundingly based on libertarian principles and clearly set out in its Declaration of Independence and formal Constitution, served as a beacon to oppressed minorities elsewhere. The American Revolution undoubtedly emboldened the disaffected in France, whose own revolution, initiated by the storming of the Bastille in July 1789 and lasting effectively until Napoleon's seizure of power ten years later, was to be the bloodiest in history. In 1793 alone, during the infamous Reign of Terror, more than 18,000 people were publicly beheaded. In the meantime, the revolutionary government (in reality a sequence of governments) was simultaneously at war with most of Europe, which justifiably feared that the revolution might spread beyond French borders.

Science and Technology

The eighteenth century was a veritable festival of exploration and discovery, in medicine, mechanics, physics, chemistry and many other fields, including weaponry. Here, as elsewhere, ingenuity sometimes outstripped practicality, as in the ill-fated, one-man, hand-cranked Turtle submarine launched into the depths off the east coast of America in 1755. More useful was Harrison's marine chronometer of 1735, which enabled sailors to pinpoint their exact position at sea; more lethal were Wilkinson's precision-boring cannon of 1774 and Bushnell's invention of the torpedo in 1777. On more peaceable fronts, the period saw the discovery and first use of electricity, most famously by Benjamin Franklin, inventor of the lightning conductor, and the Italian Alessandro Volta, who invented the electrical battery and whose surname, minus the 'a', has long since become a household word. Another similarly honoured was James Watt, whose improvement of Newcomen's steam engine in 1764 precipitated the Industrial Revolution (the term 'watt', incidentally, refers to a unit of power rather than to anything exclusively electrical). Other notable inventions include Claude Chappe's telegraph (a mechanical form of semaphore used to relay coded messages over long distances) and the hydraulic press.

Religion

Religion, as ever, remained both inspirational and contentious. Though there were signs of increased tolerance in certain quarters – as in England, which saw the founding of Methodism by John Wesley in the 1730s and of the Shaker sect in 1772, and, rather surprisingly, in Russia, where Catherine the Great granted freedom of worship in 1766 – religious bigotry continued to flourish, particularly in the relations of Protestants and Roman Catholics. The year 1731 saw the expulsion of 20,000 Protestants from Salzburg (most of whom emigrated to America), while the Jacobite rising in the mid-1740s, like the viciously anti-Catholic Gordon Riots of 1780, demonstrated the limits of religious tolerance in Britain. Nor was the appeal in 1781 by the German philosopher

Moses Mendelssohn (grandfather of the composer Felix) for better treatment of the Jews either the first or the last. While not as widespread as in the previous century, superstition was still rife amongst the less-educated classes throughout the western world.

Ideas

The eighteenth century, following on from the rationalist trends of the seventeenth, was the age of the Enlightenment, one of the richest eras in the history of western philosophy. Thinkers in every sphere of endeavour, influenced by the quickening flood of scientific discovery, placed ever greater faith in reason as the gateway to truth and natural justice. Highly critical of the *status quo* and hostile to religion, which they saw as enslaving humanity with the chains of superstition, their writings reached a wide audience and contributed directly to the underlying ideals of the American and French Revolutions. Though based mainly in France, where its principal proponents were Diderot, Voltaire and Rousseau, the movement attracted other important thinkers, most notably the Scots David Hume and Adam Smith, the American Thomas Paine and the Germans Immanuel Kant and Gotthold Lessing. Voltaire and Rousseau, in particular, used satire as a potent political weapon, and Diderot presided over one of the greatest works of scholarship ever produced: the twenty-eight-volume *Encyclopédie*, inspired by the English encyclopedia published by Ephraim Chambers in 1728 and including seventeen volumes of text and eleven of illustration. Rousseau's *Discourses on the Origins of Inequality* (1754) pilloried the decadent effects of civilisation and proclaimed the superiority of the 'noble savage'. His *Social Contract* of 1762 emphasised the rights of people over government and exhorted people everywhere to overthrow all governments not representing the genuine will of the population. Both books are among the most influential ever written. Adam

Smith was an economist whose great work *The Wealth of Nations* (1776) took the revolutionary step of defining wealth in terms of labour, and advocating individual enterprise and free trade as essentials of a just society. Hume's best-known philosophical work, *A Treatise of Human Nature* (1740), is an attack on traditional metaphysics and suggests that all true knowledge resides in personal experience. Kant, on the other hand, argued that right action cannot be based on feelings, inclinations or mere experience but only on a law given by reason, the so-called 'categorical imperative'. The subject of Thomas Paine's famous book *The Rights of Man* is self-explanatory.

The Arts

The eighteenth century saw the birth and early development of the modern novel with the works of Daniel Defoe (*Robinson Crusoe, Moll Flanders*) and Samuel Richardson (*Pamela, Clarissa*). Above all, however, it was a century of great poets. From the 1770s Goethe, Schiller and other German poets sowed the seeds of the Romantic movement which was to find its musical manifestation in the nineteenth century. They were followed chronologically by the Britons Blake, Wordsworth and Coleridge. But it was also the century of the great philosopher-satirists, of whom the greatest were Voltaire (*Candide*), Swift (*Gulliver's Travels*) and Rousseau (see above). Satire was also conspicuous in the realm of painting, as in the work of William Hogarth (*The Rake's Progress*). The greater painters and sculptors were among the finest portraitists who ever lived: David, Gainsborough, Reynolds, Chardin (who prophetically turned his attentions away from the upper classes and painted the lower bourgeoisie and working classes), Goya (whose grimly apocalyptic visions came in the next century) and Houdon, whose sculptures of Voltaire, Jefferson and Washington seem almost eerily lifelike. Amongst the century's greatest scholars and men of letters was Samuel Johnson, whose monumental *Dictionary of the English Language* (1755) was the first ever compiled. In the realm of dance, the eighteenth century saw the rise of modern ballet, centred, like so much else, in France. The most influential figures were the ballerina Marie-Anne Camargo (who in 1720 took the revolutionary step of shortening the traditional flowing, court-style dresses to reveal the feet and legs), the choreographer Jean-Georges Noverre (Mozart provided music for his *Les Petits Riens*) and the composer Jean-Philippe Rameau.

Architecture

Except in the upper reaches of society, domestic architecture in eighteenth-century Europe changed relatively little. Public buildings and the dwellings of the well-to-do changed dramatically, on both sides of the Atlantic. The grandiose and ornate gestures of the Baroque era gave way to simpler styles, many of them strongly influenced by the graceful majesty of Classical Greek and Roman designs. Famous examples are the White House and Capitol building of Washington D.C., 'Monticello', Thomas Jefferson's home in Virginia (designed by himself), and the Royal Crescent at Bath in England. With the proliferation of new cities spawned by the Industrial Revolution, and the steady expansion of the United States, architects and town planners turned their attentions to the design of not only buildings but towns and cities themselves. The gridiron pattern of Manhattan Island in New York is the fruit of just such planning, and was to be duplicated in many American cities. Here the regularity and symmetry of the neo-Classical approach had a thoroughly practical purpose: with this scheme, cities could be indefinitely extended in any direction. A striking feature of industrial architecture, in particular, was the use of new materials such as cast-iron.

Music

The eighteenth century saw the culmination of the Baroque in the great works of Bach and Handel, and the finest flowering of the Classical era which succeeded it. Domenico Scarlatti was the exact contemporary of Bach and Handel; but such was the astounding originality and exotic nature of the keyboard sonatas which have kept his name alive that he stands largely outside mainstream trends and developments. In some respects, his most important music is closer in spirit and style to the nineteenth-century Romantics than to anything else written in his own time. If the defining feature of the Baroque style (or, to be more accurate, the Baroque family of styles) was a combination of grandiosity and counterpoint (see Glossary) with a high degree of ornamentation, the Classical style represents an era whose relative simplicity of harmony, texture and style was entirely in keeping with the ascent of the middle class and the progressive weakening of the aristocracy. The learned, long-lined contrapuntal weaves of the Baroque gave way to the more straightforward texture of melody and accompaniment, the latter often simple broken chords in a pattern known as the Alberti bass (see Glossary); and the basic harmonic vocabulary became much simplified. Most music written in the Classical era (roughly 1750–1820) is based on an economical framework of four or five basic chords (triads; see Glossary) and draws its material from two or three relatively short, self-contained melodic 'themes', frequently of a simple, folk-like character. Not only themes but phrases tend to become shorter and more regular than in most Baroque music. Large-scale structures, too, become generally clearer and more symmetrical, showing analogies with the Classical architecture of the ancient Greeks and Romans. Along with a somewhat ritualised approach to form comes a more formal, more 'objective' approach to the expression of emotion. It is often easier to describe the contour of a Classical theme than it is to associate it with a particular mood. The prevailing virtues are symmetry, order, refinement and grace. The most significant contribution of the Classical era to the history of music is the crystallisation of sonata form (see Glossary), brought to its highest peak by Mozart, Haydn and Beethoven. Virtually all the great works of the Classical era are based on it. The principal genres of the period – sonata, string quartet, concerto and symphony – are all, in fact, sonatas, differing only in the size and character of the chosen instrumental medium. Standing largely apart from this development is the parallel evolution of opera, dominated in the first half of the century by Handel and Rameau and in the latter by Mozart and Gluck (1714–1787). Because he confined himself for the most part to opera, Gluck's name tends to get left out when people refer loosely to the Classical era; but he was one of the giants. His greatness lies in the quality of his music, but his long-term significance derives from his radical reforms. These did much to simplify and purify an art which had become overladen with irrelevant conventions, complicated by labyrinthine love plots, and disfigured by an excessive attention to virtuosity for its own sake. He derived his plots from classical Greek mythology (*Orfeo ed Euridice, Iphigénie en Aulide, Armide*, etc.), fashioned the music to the emotional and dramatic requirements of his libretto, softened the distinction between recitative and aria (see Glossary), paid scrupulous attention to subtleties of character development, and elevated the role of the chorus (another nod to the classical Greeks). Mozart, despite producing operas that many consider to be the greatest ever written, was not fundamentally a reformer.

Personalities

Adamberger, Johann Valentin (1740–1804): Bavarian tenor, who sang Belmonte in *The Abduction from the Seraglio* and Herr Vogelsang in *The Impresario*. A fellow-mason, he sang in Mozart's *Die Maurerfreude*, K.471. Mozart also wrote for him the arias *Per pietà, non ricercate*, K.420 and *Misero! o sogno*, K.431.

Adlgasser, Anton Cajetan (1729–1777): Composer and organist at Salzburg, he collaborated with Mozart and Michael Haydn in 1767 on the oratorio *Die Schuldigkeit des ersten Gebots*, K.35. Mozart, who greatly admired him, succeeded him as organist at Salzburg Cathedral in 1777.

Albrechtsberger, Johann Georg (1736–1809): Composer, theorist, singer and organist, he befriended Mozart and succeeded him as assistant Kapellmeister at St Stephen's Cathedral. He is best remembered today as a teacher of Beethoven in Vienna, and for having pronounced at the beginning of their association that Beethoven would 'never amount to anything'.

Attwood, Thomas (1765–1838): English composer and organist who studied with Mozart in Vienna from 1785 to 1787, keeping as mementos a number of exercise books which afford a rare insight into Mozart's teaching methods. In 1796 he became organist of St Paul's Cathedral and composer to the Chapel Royal.

Auernhammer, Josepha Barbara von (1758–1820): A highly gifted pianist, she studied with Mozart in the early 1780s and fell in love with him (unrequitedly; indeed, he wrote offensively to his father about her unprepossessing appearance). His violin sonatas K.376, 296, 377, 378, 379 and 380 are dedicated to her, and it was for her that he composed his brilliant Sonata in D for two pianos, K.448.

Bach, Johann Christian (1735–1782): The youngest son of J.S. Bach, he broke with family tradition by spending eight years in Italy, where he converted to Roman Catholicism and became a fluent and popular master of Italian opera. In 1762 he moved to London, where he remained for the rest of his life and played a major part in establishing the tradition of public concerts. He befriended the Mozarts during their London visit of 1764–5, and Mozart loved the man and admired his music to the end of his days. His earliest symphonies were strongly influenced by J.C. Bach's; indeed, he had a formative influence on Mozart's overall style, not least in his piano concertos. The slow movement of Mozart's Concerto in A major, K.414 is based on a theme of J.C. Bach's and was written in his memory.

Baglioni, Antonio: A Roman tenor, he created the roles of Don Ottavio in Mozart's *Don Giovanni* and Tito in *La clemenza di Tito*.

Barisani, Johann Joseph (1756–1826): Salzburg-born doctor of Italian origin, he became a close friend of Mozart's and attended him professionally in both Salzburg and Vienna.

Barrington, Hon. Daines (1727–1800): Nobly born English barrister who gave up the law to devote himself to the study of music and other pursuits. In 1765 he gave the nine-year-old Mozart an exhaustive examination in score-reading, sight-singing and improvisation, reporting on them to the Royal Society in 1770 and confirming his prodigious achievements and abilities.

Bassi, Luigi (1766–1825): Italian baritone who sang in the first Prague performance of *The Marriage of Figaro* and created the title role in *Don Giovanni*. He remained an authoritative and popular champion of Mozart's music.

Beecke, Notger Ignaz Franz von (1733–1803): German composer and keyboard virtuoso who 'competed' with Mozart in a friendly contest in Mannheim in the winter of 1774–5. The two met again in 1777 and in 1790, when they played a concerto together.

Beethoven, Ludwig van (1770–1827): Later the greatest composer of his age, he came to Vienna in April 1787 as a youth of sixteen, hoping to study with Mozart, though whether he actually had any lessons is unknown. He certainly played for him, and Mozart allegedly declared that he 'would make a great noise in the world'. He was deeply influenced by Mozart's music. As a pianist he gave public performances of Mozart's Concerto in D minor, K.466 and wrote for it the cadenzas still generally played today.

Benucci, Francesco (1745–1824): Italian bass-baritone who created the title role in *The Marriage of Figaro* and the role of Guglielmo in *Così fan tutte*, and sang Leporello in the first Viennese performance of *Don Giovanni*.

Bullinger, Franz Joseph Johann Nepomuk (1744–1810): A lifelong friend of the Mozarts, he was a Jesuit priest employed as a tutor in Salzburg. It was to him that Mozart first confided that his mother had died in 1778, asking him to prepare Leopold and Nannerl for the news.

Bussani, Francesco (1743–after 1807): Italian bass. He stage-managed the premiere of Mozart's *The Impresario* in Vienna and doubled as Bartolo and Antonio in the premiere of *The Marriage of Figaro*, and as the Commendatore and Masetto in the first Viennese production of *Don Giovanni*, as well as playing Don Alfonso in the first performance of *Così fan tutte*. His wife, Dorothea, was the first Cherubino in *Figaro* and the first Despina in *Così fan tutte*.

Cannabich, Christian (1731–1798): German violinist and composer, from a distinguished family of musicians, he was Konzertmeister and director of instrumental music at the Mannheim court, moving with the court to Munich in 1778. He and his family were great friends to Mozart and his mother during their stay in Mannheim in 1777–8. His daughter Rosa became a pupil of Mozart's and it was for her that he wrote the Piano Sonata in C, K.309.

Cavalieri, Catarina (1755–1801): Italian-born soprano much admired by Mozart, she was the first Constanze in *The Abduction from the Seraglio*, the first Mlle Silberklang in *The Impresario*, and sang Elvira in the first Viennese performance of *Don Giovanni* and the Countess in the 1789 revival of *Figaro*.

Clementi, Muzio (1752–1832): Italian-born (later English) composer, piano manufacturer, and one of the most original and influential pianists of his time. He competed with Mozart in a famous contest at the Viennese court of Joseph II in 1781.

Da Ponte, Lorenzo (1749–1838): Italian librettist of Mozart's three finest comedies, *The Marriage of Figaro*, *Don Giovanni* and *Così fan tutte*. A peripatetic poet and notorious womaniser, he worked in various cities, including Vienna, London and New York. He also worked with Salieri and Martín y Soler.

Dittersdorf, Carl Ditters von (1739–1799): Esteemed German composer. He played second violin in string quartets with Haydn, Vanhal and Mozart in Vienna.

Duschek, Franz Xaver (1731–1799): Settled in Prague in 1770 and made his name as a pianist, teacher and composer, mainly of orchestral and instrumental music. He and his wife Josepha became close friends of the Mozarts. It was at their villa near Prague that Wolfgang completed *Don Giovanni.* Josepha and Mozart are believed by some biographers to have had an affair.

Eybler, Joseph Leopold (1765–1846): Austrian composer, a pupil of Albrechtsberger and Haydn. He became a close friend of Mozart and helped in rehearsing the first production of *Così fan tutte.* Mozart's widow commissioned him to complete her husband's Requiem, though it was largely Mozart's pupil Süssmayr who eventually did the job. Eybler succeeded Salieri as Kapellmeister at the Austrian court, but resigned in 1833 after suffering a stroke while conducting Mozart's Requiem.

Galitzin, Prince Dmitry Michailovich (1721–1793): Russian Ambassador in Vienna, he was one of Mozart's chief patrons in 1784.

Grimm, Baron Friedrich Melchior von (1723–1807): German diplomat and secretary to the Duke of Orleans in Paris, where he was Mozart's most influential champion in 1763–4, 1766 and 1778. He left fascinating accounts of the child Mozart and his manipulative father.

Haibel, Sophie (*née* Weber) (1763–1846): Mozart's sister-in-law, the youngest daughter of Fridolin Weber, she married the composer and singer Jakob Haibel. After his death she went to live in Salzburg with her sister Constanze.

Hasse, Johann Adolf (1699–1783): The most successful opera composer of his time. Mozart met him in Vienna in 1769 and again in Milan in 1771, when the fifteen-year-old's *Ascanio in Alba* followed (and eclipsed) Hasse's *Ruggiero*.

Haydn, Joseph (1732–1809): With Mozart and Beethoven, one of the three great pillars of the Classical era in music. He first met Mozart in 1781 and the two became fast friends and deep admirers of each other's work. Haydn played the violin at quartet meetings with Mozart, Vanhal and Dittersdorf, and it was to him that Mozart dedicated his six quartets K.387, 421, 428, 458, 464 and 465.

Haydn, Michael (1737–1806): German composer, brother of Joseph. Entered service of the Archbishop of Salzburg in 1762, where he afterwards became organist. Mozart famously wrote two masterpieces (the duos for violin and viola) for Haydn to pass off as his own.

Kelly, Michael (1762–1826): Irish tenor. Became friendly with Mozart in Vienna and created the roles of Don Curzio and Basilio in *Figaro*. His *Reminiscences* shed fascinating light on Mozart and musical life in Vienna.

Lange, Aloysia (*née* Weber) (1761–1839): Brilliant German soprano. Mozart fell in love with her during his visit to Mannheim in 1777 and wrote several arias for her. She did not reciprocate his feelings and married the actor Joseph Lange in Vienna; two years later Mozart married her sister Constanze. Aloysia and her husband were close friends of the Mozarts – her husband's unfinished portrait of Mozart is perhaps the most familiar of all and now hangs in the Mozart Museum in Salzburg.

Leutgeb, Joseph Ignaz (1732–1811): Austrian horn player, and a lifelong friend of Mozart's. In 1777 he moved from Salzburg to Vienna, where he ran a cheesemonger's shop and continued his musical career. Mozart's horn concertos were written for him.

Martini, Giovanni Battista (1706–1784): Franciscan monk, composer, theorist and *maestro di cappella* at the church of San Francesco, Bologna. He was a famous teacher. Mozart studied with him briefly in Bologna in 1770, and described him in a letter as 'the one person in the world whom I love, revere and esteem most of all'.

Mesmer, Franz Anton (1734–1815): German doctor, famous for his method of healing by 'animal magnetism' (parodied by Mozart in *Così fan tutte*). He was a great music lover and amateur musician, and it was in the garden of his home in Vienna that the child Mozart's *Bastien und Bastienne* was first performed.

Mozart, Carl Thomas (1784–1858): Mozart's second son, and the first to survive to adulthood. He trained as a musician but later gave up music and took a position in the service of the viceroy.

Mozart, Constanze (*née* Weber) (1762–1842): Mozart's wife. Of their six children, only two survived infancy. After Mozart's death Constanze organised and sang in several performances of his works. In 1809 she married G.N. Nissen, with whom she wrote a biography of Mozart.

Mozart, Franz Xaver Wolfgang (1791–1844): Youngest of Mozart's children. He studied music with Hummel and Salieri, and like his father was a musical prodigy, publishing a piano quintet when he was eleven. His compositions include piano concertos, chamber and solo piano music, and a number of songs.

Mozart, Leopold (1719–1787): Mozart's father. He was intended for a career in the church but defied his parents and went into music instead, entering the service of the Archbishop of Salzburg and rising to become vice-Kapellmeister. Of his seven children, only two, Maria Anna (Nannerl) and Wolfgang, survived infancy. His compositions, including several masses and other church pieces, numerous symphonies and concertos, and a good many chamber works, have been overshadowed by those of his son; but his *Versuch einer gründlichen Violinschule* (1756) remains one of the most important instrumental treatises ever written.

Mozart, Maria Anna (known as 'Nannerl') (1751–1829): Mozart's sister. A phenomenally gifted keyboard player, she toured Europe with her family. In 1784 she married the magistrate Johann Baptist Franz von Berchtold zu Sonnenburg, where her son (whom she handed over to her father to raise as his own) and two daughters were born. After her husband's death in 1801 she returned to Salzburg, earning her living as a piano teacher.

Mozart, Maria Anna Thekla (1758–1841): Mozart's cousin (known as 'the Bäsle'), the daughter of Leopold's brother Franz. In 1784 she gave birth to an illegitimate daughter, Josepha; the father was later identified as Abbé Theodor Franz von Reibeld (1752–1807), a canon at Augsburg Cathedral.

Paradies (Paradis), Maria Theresia von (1759–1824): Blind Austrian pianist and composer. Mozart's Piano Concerto No. 18 in B flat, K.456 was probably written for her.

Ployer, Barbara von (also known as 'Babette'): Daughter of an agent of the Salzburg court in Vienna. She was a pupil of Mozart, who wrote two of his finest piano concertos (K.449, 453) for her.

Ramm, Friedrich (1744–1811): Oboist in the court orchestra at Mannheim, and a close companion of Mozart, both in Mannheim and in Paris. Mozart's Oboe Quartet in F, K.370 was written for him.

Rauzzini, Venanzio (1746–1810): Italian castrato singer. Mozart composed for him the part of Cecilio in *Lucio Silla*, K.135 (1772) and the virtuoso solo motet, *Exsultate, jubilate*, K.165.

Salieri, Antonio (1750–1825): Famous Italian composer. In 1788 he was appointed Kapellmeister at Vienna, and most of his church pieces were composed for the Viennese court. He also wrote many operas and much chamber music. Many famous musicians, including Beethoven, Schubert and Liszt, were among his pupils. The popular suspicion that he poisoned Mozart is wholly without foundation.

Schachtner, Johann Andreas (1731–1795): Salzburg-based Austrian trumpeter, violinist, cellist and writer. He has left charming accounts of Mozart as a child. He translated the librettos of *La finta giardiniera*, K.196 and *Idomeneo*, K.366 into German and wrote the text of Mozart's *Zaide*, K.344.

Schikaneder, Emanuel (1751–1812): Austrian actor and impresario. He wrote the libretto of *The Magic Flute*, in which he also played the role of Papageno.

Stadler, Anton Paul (1753–1812): Brilliant clarinettist and basset-horn player. He was renowned for his playing in the low register of the clarinet and devised a downward extension of the instrument. It was for this – the basset clarinet – that Mozart composed his Clarinet Quintet, K.581 and Clarinet Concerto, K.622. Impecunious, he freely borrowed money from Mozart when the composer was himself in financial difficulties.

Süssmayr, Franz Xaver (1766–1803): Austrian composer, a pupil of both Salieri and Mozart. After Mozart's death he became a successful opera composer, and from 1794 until his death he worked at the National Theatre in Vienna. He completed the Requiem, K.626 and, more modestly, the Horn Concerto No. 1 in D major, K.412 that Mozart left unfinished at his death.

Vanhal, Johann Baptist (1739–1813): Czech composer. Though suffering from an intermittent mental illness, he composed prolifically and played the cello in string quartets with Mozart, Haydn and Dittersdorf.

Weber, Franz Fridolin (1733–1779): German musician active at the Mannheim court as a violinist, singer and copyist. Of his four daughters, the third, Constanze, became Mozart's wife, but only after Fridolin's death.

Selected Bibliography

Anderson, Emily, ed. and trans., *Letters of Mozart and his Family*, London, 1938; third edition, prepared by Stanley Sadie and Fiona Smart, London, 1988

Biancolli, Louis, ed., *The Mozart Handbook*, New York, 1962

Blom, Eric, *Mozart*, London, 1935; rev. 1962

Braunbehrens, Volkmar, *Mozart in Vienna, 1781–1791*, London, 1989

Brophy, Brigid, *Mozart the Dramatist*, London, 1964; rev. edition, New York, 1990

Burk, J. N., *Mozart and his Music*, New York, 1959

Carr, Francis, *Mozart and Constanze*, London, 1983

Da Ponte, Lorenzo, *Memoirs*, trans. L.A. Shepherd, London, 1929; rev. edition, New York, 1959

Davidson, Michael, *Mozart and the Pianist*, London, 2001

Davies, Peter J., *Mozart in Person: His Character and Health*, New York, 1989

Dent, Edward J., *Mozart's Operas*, Oxford, 1947

Deutsch, Otto Erich, *Mozart – A Documentary Biography*, rev. edition, London, 1966

Einstein, Alfred, *Mozart: His Character, His Work*, Oxford, 1962

Eisen, Cliff, *New Mozart Documents*, Stanford, 1991
                - *Mozart Studies*, New York, 1991

Girdlestone, C. M., *Mozart and His Piano Concertos*, Paris, 1939; rev. edition, New York, 1964

Gutman, Robert W., *Mozart: A Cultural Biography*, New York, 1999

Heartz, Daniel, *Mozart's Operas*, Berkeley, 1990
                - *Haydn, Mozart and the Viennese School 1740–1780*, New York, 1995

Hildesheimer, Wolfgang, *Mozart*, New York, 1982

Hussey, Dyneley, *Wolfgang Amadeus Mozart*, London, 1928

Hutchings, Arthur, *A Companion to Mozart's Piano Concertos*, Oxford, 1950
                - *Mozart – The Man, the Musician*, New York, 1976

Jahn, Otto, *W.A. Mozart*, Leipzig, 1866–9; Eng. trans. as *Life of Mozart*, London, 1891

Kerman, Joseph, *Opera as Drama*, New York, 1956

King, A.H., *Mozart in Retrospect – Studies in Criticism and Bibliography*, Oxford, 1955
                - *Mozart – a Biography with a Survey of Books*, London, 1956

Landon, H.C. Robbins, *Mozart's Last Year*, London, 1988
                - *Mozart: The Golden Years*, London, 1989
                - *The Mozart Compendium*, London, 1990
                - *Mozart and Vienna*, London, 1991
                - *Mozart Essays*, New York, 1995

Levey, Michael, *The Life and Death of Mozart*, London, 1971

Loesser, Arthur, *Men, Women and Pianos – A Social History*, New York, 1954

Newman, Ernest, *Great Operas*, London, 1958

Osborne, Charles, *The Complete Operas of Mozart: A Critical Guide*, London, 1978

Ottaway, Hugh, *Mozart*, London, 1979

Rosen, Charles, *The Classical Style – Haydn, Mozart, Beethoven*, New York, 1972

Sadie, Stanley, *Mozart*, London, 1966
                - *The New Grove Mozart*, London, 1982

Solomon, Maynard, *Mozart – A Life*, London, 1995

Spaethling, Robert, trans., *Mozart's Letters, Mozart's Life: Selected Letters*, New York, 2000

Stafford, William, *Mozart's Death*, London, 1991
                - *The Mozart Myths: A Critical Reassessment*, Stanford, 1991

Steptoe, Andrew, *The Mozart–Da Ponte Operas*, Oxford, 1988

Till, Nicholas, *Mozart and the Enlightenment: Truth, Virtue and Beauty in Mozart's Operas*, New York, 1993

Turner, W. J., *Mozart: The Man and his Works*, New York, 1938

Tyson, Alan, *Mozart. Studies of the Autograph Scores*, Harvard, 1987

Zaslaw, Neil, *Mozart's Symphonies: Context, Performance Practice, Reception*, London, 1989

Glossary

Adagio Slow.

Alberti bass A stylised accompaniment popular in the later eighteenth century, and based on the triad, which is spelt out in the order bottom–top–middle–top (as in C–G–E–G etc.). This and many other forms of triadic variation are almost omnipresent in Mozart's piano music.

Allegro Fast, but not excessively so.

Alto The second-highest voice in a four-part choir.

Andante Slowish, at a moderate walking pace.

Aria Solo song (also called 'air'), generally as part of an opera or oratorio, though there are many free-standing 'concert arias' and self-contained operatic scenas, of which most of the greatest are by Mozart. The aria has a ternary (A–B–A) design in which the third part duplicates (and usually embellishes) the first, and is often called a 'da capo' aria.

Bar (US: Measure) The visual division of metre into successive units, marked off on the page by vertical lines (barlines).

Cadence A coming to rest on a particular note or key, as in the standard 'Amen' at the end of a hymn.

Cadenza A relatively brief, often showy solo of improvisatory character in the context of a concerto, operatic aria, or other orchestral form. In concertos it usually heralds the orchestral close to a movement (generally the first movement).

Cantata A work in several movements (arias, recitatives, duets, etc.) for accompanied voice or voices on a smaller scale than an oratorio (from the Latin *cantare*, to sing). Mozart wrote six cantatas: K.42, 429, 469 (largely arranged from the great C minor Mass), 471, 619 and (his final completed work) 623, of which the last three have Masonic associations.

Coda An extra section following the expected close of a movement, often including a rousing (and sometimes extensive) final flourish.

Codetta A small coda.

Concerto A work usually for solo instrument and orchestra, generally in three movements (fast–slow–fast). The first movement is usually in sonata form (see below). All Mozart's concertos are of this type; many of them are among the finest examples ever penned.

Concord · A euphonious combination of notes. The opposite of discord.

Counterpoint, contrapuntal · The interweaving of separate 'horizontal' melodic lines, as opposed to the accompaniment of a top-line ('horizontal') melody by a series of ('vertical') chords.

Development · The middle section in sonata form (see below), usually characterised by modulation (see below) through several new keys.

Dynamics · The gradations of softness and loudness, and the terms which indicate them (*pianissimo, fortissimo*, etc.).

Exposition · The first section in sonata form (see below), in which the main themes and their relationships are first presented.

Fantasy, fantasia · A free form, often of an improvisatory nature, following the composer's fancy rather than any pre-ordained structures. Mozart's fantasias include three for the piano (K.396, 397 & 475) and one composed for mechanical organ (K.608). There are some later fantasies, however, like Schubert's *Wanderer Fantasy* and Schumann's Fantasia in C, both for piano, which are tightly integrated works incorporating fully fledged sonata forms, scherzos, fugues, etc.

Finale · A generic term for 'last movement'.

Forte, fortissimo · Loud, very loud.

Fortepiano · The name given to the early pianos known to Mozart. Their sound is similar to a cross between a harpsichord and a harp.

Fugue · An imitative work in several overlapping parts or 'voices' (the term applies irrespective of whether the fugue is vocal or instrumental). Fugue derives from the same principle as the common round, though it can be immeasurably more complicated. More of a technique than a fixed form, it begins with a solo tune (known as the 'subject'). On the completion of this tune (or melodic fragment – there are some fugues based on a mere four notes), the second voice enters with an 'answer' (the same tune, but in a different, complementary key). While the second voice is presenting the theme ('subject'), the first continues with a new tune (known as a 'countersubject'). In the overlapping scheme of things this is equivalent to the second phrase of a round or canon ('Dormez-vous?' in *Frère Jacques*, 'See how they run' in *Three Blind Mice*). When subject and countersubject complete their dovetailed counterpoint, another 'voice' enters with its own statement of the subject. Voice two now repeats voice one's countersubject, while voice one introduces a new countersubject. And so it goes, alternating with 'episodes' in which the various voices combine in free counterpoint, but with no full statements of the subject in any voice. Mozart wrote a number of fugues, the finest of which include the Fugue in C minor, K.426 for two pianos (later arranged for strings), the 'Cum sancto spiritu' from the C minor Mass, K.427, and the Kyrie from the Requiem, K.626. The finale of the 'Jupiter' Symphony is a superb amalgam of fugue and sonata form (see below).

Harmony   The simultaneous sounding of notes to make a chord. Harmonies (chords) often serve as expressive or atmospheric 'adjectives', describing or giving added meaning to the notes of a melody, which, in turn, might be likened to nouns and verbs.

Harpsichord   A keyboard instrument in which the strings are plucked rather than struck.

Interval   The distance in pitch between two notes, heard either simultaneously or successively. The sounding of the first two notes of a scale is therefore described as a major or minor 'second', the sounding of the first and third notes a major or minor 'third', etc.

Key   See 'Tonality', below.

Legato   Smooth, connected, the sound of one note 'touching' the sound of the next; as though in one breath.

Major   See 'Modes', below.

Metre, metrical   The grouping together of beats in recurrent units of two, three, four, six, etc. Metre is the pulse of music.

Minor   See 'Modes', below.

Minuet, menuet   A French dance, originating in the folk tradition. It can be seen as an ancestor of the waltz, sharing with it the triple metre and moderate tempo, and an elegance born of long cultivation by the royal courts of Europe. It became one of the most popular optional dances of the Baroque suite (examples abound in Bach) and is the only one to have survived the suite's decline in the middle of the eighteenth century. Mozart's minuets are too numerous to mention individually. An exception, though, should be made for the D major Minuet, K.355, for solo piano, which in its extraordinary chromaticism is one of his most advanced and prophetic pieces.

Modes   The names given to the particular arrangement of notes within a scale. Every key in western classical music has two versions: the major and the minor mode. The decisive factor is the size of the interval between the tonic note (the foundation on which scales are built) and the third degree of the scale. If it is compounded of two whole tones (as in C to E), the mode is major. If the third tone is made up of one and a half tones (C to E flat), the mode is minor. In general, the minor mode is darker and more 'serious' than the major. The church modes prevalent in the Middle Ages comprise various combinations of major and minor and are less dynamically 'directed' in character. These appear only rarely in music after the Baroque era (c. 1600–1750) and have generally been used by composers to create some kind of archaic effect.

Modulation   The movement from one key to another, generally involving at least one pivotal chord common to both keys. Modulation is thus a major component in the alternation of stability and flux, which is the bedrock of sonata form (see below) and accounts for most of Mozart's extended works.

Motif, motive   A kind of musical acorn. A melodic or rhythmical figure too brief to constitute a proper theme, but one on which themes are built. A perfect example is the beginning of Beethoven's Fifth Symphony: ta-ta-ta dah; ta-ta-ta dah.

Obbligato   A term for indicating the compulsory use of an instrument in a context where such a role is not normally expected.

Octave   The simultaneous sounding of any note with its nearest namesake, up or down (C to C, F to F, etc.). The effect is an enrichment, through increased mass and variety of pitch, without any increase of harmonic tension.

Oratorio   An extended choral/orchestral setting of religious texts in a dramatic and semi-operatic fashion. Mozart's only true oratorio, *La Betulia liberata*, K.118, was composed in 1771, when he was fifteen, and is a relatively minor work. The most famous of all oratorios is Handel's *Messiah*.

Phrase   A smallish group of notes (generally accommodated by the exhalation of a single breath) which forms a unit of melody, as in 'God save our Gracious Queen...' and 'My Country, 'tis of thee...'

Phrasing   The shaping of music into phrases.

Piano, pianissimo   Soft, very soft.

Pianoforte   The full name of the piano, now regarded as archaic, as in 'violoncello' for the cello.

Pizzicato   Plucked strings.

Polyphony	Music with two or more interweaving melodic strands.
Prelude	Literally, a piece which precedes and introduces another piece (as in the standard 'Prelude and Fugue'). However, the name has been applied (most famously by Bach, Chopin and Debussy) to describe free-standing short pieces, often of a semi-improvisatory nature. Mozart composed his own preludes to a number of fugues from J.S. Bach's *Well-Tempered Clavier*.
Recapitulation	The third and final section in sonata form (see below), where the ideas of the exposition return in the home key. Recapitulations often also involve fresh thematic development.
Recitative	A short narrative section especially characteristic of Baroque and Classical opera and oratorio. It is normally sung by a solo voice accompanied by continuo chords, and usually precedes an aria. The rhythm is in a free style, being dictated by the words. Many of Mozart's recitatives are among the most lively and psychologically insightful ever written.
Resolution	When a suspension or dissonance comes to rest on a concord.
Ritornello	A theme or section for orchestra recurring in different keys between solo passages in an aria or concerto.
Rondo	A movement in which the main theme announced at the beginning makes repeated appearances, interspersed with contrasting sections known as 'episodes'. At its simplest (when the episodes are more or less identical) the form can be summarised by the formula A–B–A–B–A. In most rondos, though, the episodes are different in each case: A–B–A–C–A. There are also many rondos with more episodes (A–B–A–C–A–D–A etc.). The form appears both as a self-contained work in its own right and as a movement (usually the last) of a sonata, symphony, or concerto. Mozart's rondos are almost all to be found in the context of larger works; but he did write a number of free-standing examples, including three for solo piano (K.485, 494 & 511), two for piano and orchestra (K.382 & 386), and two for violin and orchestra (K.269 & 373).
Scale	From the Italian word *scala* ('ladder'). A series of adjacent, 'stepwise' notes (A–B–C–D–E–F etc.), moving up or down. These 'ladders' provide the basic cast of characters from which melodies are made and keys established.
Sonata form	Also known as 'sonata-allegro' and 'first-movement' form, this was the dominant form throughout the second half of the eighteenth century and the first third of the nineteenth. It is basically a ternary (three-part)

design in which the last part is a modified repeat of the first (deriving from the *da capo* aria), but with one very important difference: while the first section is cast in two contrasting keys, the third remains predominantly in the key of the tonic (the key of the movement as a whole).

The three sections of the standard sonata form are called exposition, development and recapitulation. The exposition, which may be prefaced by a slow introduction, is based on the complementary tensions of two 'opposing' keys. Each key group generally has its own themes, but this contrast is of secondary importance (many of Haydn's sonata movements are based on a single theme, which passes through various adventures on its voyages from key to key). In movements in the major mode, the secondary key in works before 1800 is almost invariably the dominant. When the key of the movement is in the minor mode, the secondary key will almost always be the relative major. The exposition always ends in the secondary key, never on the tonic.

In many sonata-form movements, the main themes of the two key groups are of a contrasting character. If the first main theme is blustery or military, the second, in the complementary key, is often more lyrical.

The development is altogether more free and unpredictable. In most cases, true to its name, it takes themes or ideas from the exposition and 'develops' them; or it may ignore the themes of the exposition altogether, as Mozart often does. What it will have is a notably increased sense of harmonic instability, drifting, or in some cases struggling, through a number of different keys before delivering us back to the tonic for the recapitulation. Since the recapitulation lacks the tonal tensions of the exposition, the themes themselves, now all in the same key, take on a new relationship. In its prescribed resolution of family (tonal) conflicts, sonata form may be seen as the most Utopian of all musical structures.

Sonata   Usually a piece for solo piano, or one instrument plus piano, in three movements. The overall layout consists of a fast (or quite fast) opening movement (normally in sonata form), a central slow movement, and a quick finale (often a rondo). Sometimes there are four movements, in which case the extra one is almost always a minuet or (from Beethoven onwards) a scherzo, and the finale either in rondo or sonata form.

String quartet   A sonata for two violins, viola and cello, normally in four movements; also the name for the instrumental group itself.

String quintet   A sonata normally for string quartet with an additional viola (as in Mozart's) or (infrequently) an additional cello. It is usually in four movements.

Suspension   A note from one chord held over into a following chord of which it is not a member. The result is almost always a heightening of emotional intensity.

Symphony   A sonata for orchestra, normally in four movements.

Syncopation   Accents falling on irregular beats, generally giving a 'swinging' feel; often found in jazz.

Tempo   The speed of music.

Tonality   There is probably no aspect of music harder to describe than tonality – or 'key'. Put at its broadest, it has to do with a kind of tonal solar system in which each note ('planet'), each rung of the scale exists in a fixed and specific relationship to one particular note ('sun'), which is known as the 'key note' or 'tonic'. When this planetary system is based on the note 'C', the music is said to be 'in the key of C'. Each note of the scale has a different state of 'tension', a different degree of 'unrest' in relation to the key note; and each arouses a different degree and specificity of expectation in the listener, which the composer can either resolve or frustrate. Through the use of 'alien' notes, not present in the prevailing scale, the composer can shift from one solar system, from one 'key', to another. On the way, a sense of stability gives way to a sense of instability, of flux, which is not resolved until the arrival of the new key. This process of moving from one key to another is known as 'modulation'.

Tone colour, timbre   That property of sound which distinguishes a horn from a piano, a violin from a xylophone, etc.

Triad   A three-note chord, especially those including the root, third and fifth of a scale (C–E–G, A–C–E, etc.) in any order. (See also 'Alberti bass', above.)

Triplets   In duple metre, a grouping (or groupings) of three notes in the space of two (as in the 'Buckle-my' of 'One, Two / Buckle-my shoe').

Variation   Any decorative or otherwise purposeful alteration of a note, rhythm, timbre, etc. There are four basic types of variation:

1) Those in which the original tune is clothed in a sequence of stylistic and textural dresses (ornamental turns, decorative scale passages, rhythmic, textural and tempo alterations, and so on) while the chief outline of the melody, the original harmonies and the overall form of the theme are preserved – though the mode (major or minor) may sometimes be altered. The same techniques of variation can be applied, within the given limits, even to those elements which are retained from the original theme. The bass line, for instance, may be amplified by a trill, fast or slow, or be doubled in octaves, and the basic chords of the original harmonies may be 'seasoned' with decorative notes adjacent to those of the original. This form is known generally as melodic variation.

Almost all variation sets of the Classical period (loosely, 1750 to 1820) are of this kind, Mozart's being perhaps the best known.

2) Those in which the harmonic pattern of the theme is preserved while melody, tempo, rhythm, texture (chords or intertwining melodic lines) and mode (major/minor) may change beyond recognition.

3) Those in which the theme is not a self-sufficient melody but either a constantly reiterated bass line, above which the upper parts may change, or a series of chords, whose harmonic sequence and unvarying rhythm is reiterated, unchanged, throughout the composition. This form of variation is called both passacaglia and chaconne (in the Baroque era the two names were used interchangeably).

4) Those in which only a part of the original theme (a single melodic phrase, a motto rhythm, a structural form) is retained as a basis for variation, all other parts being subject to very considerable transformation.

Mozart's Variations on *Ah, vous dirai-je, Maman*, K.265 ('Twinkle, Twinkle, Little Star' to most of us) provide an excellent introduction to these techniques, partly because the theme is so familiar and thus easy to keep track of. They also provide an excellent example of the stereotyped layout of late eighteenth-century keyboard variations.

Annotations of CD Tracks: CD 1

1 Minuet in G, K.1

Composed when he was five, this is the earliest piece by Mozart to come down to us. As we know from Schachtner's charming anecdote, however (pp. 4–5), it was not his first attempt at composition. Nor, strictly speaking, did he actually write it. The manuscript is clearly in Leopold's hand. Though played on the piano from the moment it entered the standard teaching repertoire, it was originally played, as here, on the harpsichord. In 1761, the fortepiano's decisive conquest of the older instrument still lay some way in the future. The Mozarts did not possess a fortepiano; indeed, there may have been none anywhere in Salzburg. In its courtly grace and simplicity, the Minuet and its Trio reveal in sound the child Mozart's acute observation of the external world. As he heard, so he wrote.

2 Symphony No. 1 in E flat, K.16. **Movement 1: Molto allegro**

Scored for pairs of oboes and horns with strings and harpsichord continuo, Mozart's First Symphony (1764) is as impressive for its sure and stylish orchestration as for its musical content. In this case the model was not aristocratic dances at the Salzburg court but the symphonies of Mozart's new friend in London, Johann Christian Bach, his senior by twenty-one years. The friendship between the eight-year-old composer and his role model is one of the most touching in musical history. Mozart cherished the memory of their association, renewed briefly in Paris in 1778, throughout his life. (Bach's death in 1782, at the age of forty-six, is formally mourned in the Piano Concerto No. 12 in A major, K.414, whose slow movement is based on a theme by J.C. Bach.) The First Symphony opens with an affecting movement in straightforward sonata form. Already, Mozart shows his love of the viola in his scoring of the second main theme.

3 Piano Concerto No. 3 in D, K.40. **Finale: Presto**

The sources for this concerto are solo keyboard sonatas by L. Honauer (first movement), J.G. Eckard (middle movement) and C.P.E. Bach (finale). As with its three siblings, the solo material is left almost entirely intact, Mozart providing the orchestral introductions (ritornellos), interludes, accompaniments, and final flourishes, drawing virtually all his material from the original sonatas. Composed/arranged in 1767, when he was eleven, each of these first experiments with concerto forms and textures shows his burgeoning awareness of the medium's dramatic possibilities. It was in his concertos that he was to achieve his most sustained level of inspiration and compositional mastery.

4 Ascanio in Alba, K.111. Act I, Scene 1: Aria 'L'ombre de'rami tuoi'

Ascanio in Alba, Mozart's second full-length opera, was written in 1771, when he was fifteen. His first, *Mitridate, rè di Ponto*, had been written and produced in the previous year. At this very early stage of his operatic career, he had no say in the choice of either the plot or the librettist. The combined tedium and pretentiousness of both, in this case, would have sunk many a composer three times Mozart's age. It did not sink Mozart. Written to celebrate a royal wedding (see p. 33), the opera is laden with heavy-handed allegory. The hero, Ascanio, son of Venus, is a clear stand-in for the royal bridegroom, son of the Empress Maria Theresa. The heroine, Ascanio's fiancée Silvia, is represented as a descendant of Hercules – she being descended from Ercole (Hercules) d'Este, fifteenth-century scion of one of Italy's foremost families. Since the libretto was delivered scandalously late, Mozart was forced to compose almost the entire score in less than a month (he had written much of the Overture before the libretto's arrival). Italian opera at that time was emphatically a singer's medium. Often it consisted of a sequence of virtuoso arias in which characterisation and dramatic coherence played no part and vocal pyrotechnics predominated over musical substance. At fifteen, Mozart was not about to overturn tradition. He did as expected; but he did it extraordinarily well. In the opening scene, heard here, Venus sings the praises of Alba and proposes that Ascanio should go there as its ruler. In a ploy to test her virtue, she also advises him to adopt a false identity when introducing himself to his intended.

5 Piano Concerto No. 5 in D, K.175. **Finale: Allegro**

Mozart's first wholly original concerto (1773) pleased him so much that he kept it in his repertoire for more than a decade. Together with the *Concertone* for two violins, K.190, the Bassoon Concerto, K.191 and the First Violin Concerto, K.207, it forms a group of early concertos nourished by his experience of opera. Already it is clear that Mozart envisaged the concerto as an intrinsically dramatic medium. Throughout his career, his piano concertos and his operas seem almost to 'shadow' one another. Among his operatic innovations was a shift away from solo-dominated operas towards ensemble opera. A pointer in that direction is the contrapuntal finale of this first original piano concerto, which struck many of its initial listeners as unacceptably 'severe'. It hardly sounds that way today.

6 Symphony No. 25 in G minor, K.183. **Movement 1: Allegro con brio**

This was Mozart's 'breakthrough' symphony – the first in which he demonstrated an absolutely individual voice, and the one in which he served notice that his surprisingly long symphonic apprenticeship was over. It represents both a new level of compositional mastery and a dramatic widening of his expressive range in a purely instrumental idiom. The first and last movements, in particular, have a turbulence of spirit which parallels Haydn's so-called *Sturm und Drang* ('Storm and Stress') symphonies of the late 1760s and early 1770s. The term refers to a German literary movement which flourished briefly in the 1770s, characterised by emotional intensity and a revolt against social and artistic conventions. In this symphony, his first in a minor key, the seventeen-year-old Mozart makes his first overtly rebellious gesture, implicitly scoffing at the triviality of the *galant* style. As the British writer Eric Blom pointed out, Mozart's comparatively rare use of the minor mode often accompanies the shedding of a repression. Uncoincidentally, the *galant* style was personified by Leopold Mozart, who strongly urged it upon his son.

7 Symphony No. 29 in A, K.201. **Finale: Allegro con spirito**

This sublimely sunny A major Symphony followed the G minor Symphony (No. 40) in less than a year. In its particular combination of serenity, joy and apparently effortless mastery, it remains unique in Mozart's symphonic output. The intensity of feeling is hardly less than in the G minor, but of an almost diametrically opposite kind. The tools of the *Sturm und Drang* movement (harmonic and rhythmic restlessness, tremolando string writing, etc.) are almost as much in evidence here as in the G minor, but used to very different ends.

[8] Piano Concerto No. 9 in E flat, K.271 'Jeunehomme'. **Movement 2: Andantino**

This ground-breaking masterpiece has already been discussed at some length on pp. 94–5. The middle movement is the most overtly 'operatic' in the entire series of piano concertos. While unusual in the depth and intensity of its emotional world, it foreshadows many of Mozart's concertos in being flowing rather than truly slow. The present performance, however, is perhaps the fastest on record, so readers already familiar with the work should be prepared to suspend any preconceptions. The indicated tempo is the ambiguous *Andantino*, which has variously been interpreted as either 'a little faster' or 'a little slower' than *Andante*. At any tempo, however, the movement is one of the marvels of the repertoire.

[9] Piano Sonata in C, K.309. **Movement 2: Andante, un poco adagio**

This sonata has more than its intrinsic musical value. Composed during his stay in Mannheim in 1777, its central movement (*Andante, un poco Adagio*), as noted on page 59, is a deliberate aural portrait, the subject being Rosa Cannabich, daughter of Christian Cannabich, the Mannheim Orchestra's 'general-in-chief'. This fact alone reveals that, even in his purely instrumental music, Mozart the born opera composer saw music in terms of characterisation. It is highly unlikely that this is the only case of musical portrayal in his instrumental output. Indeed, it is reasonable to assume that most of his music is a rich gallery of undercover portraits, not merely of individuals but of humanity.

[10] Concerto in C for flute and harp, K.299. **Finale: Allegro**

A product of his generally unhappy time in Paris in 1778, this is among the most popular of all Mozart's concertos. Few would cite it as anything like his greatest. Commissioned by the Parisian diplomat and amateur flautist Comte de Guines for himself and his harpist daughter, the work gave Mozart little joy during or after its composition (quick to commission, the Comte was slow to pay up). Little can he have imagined how much pleasure this graceful and inventive music would bring to generation after generation of music lovers.

[11] Piano Sonata in A minor, K.310. **Movement 2: Andante cantabile con espressione**

For many musicians and music lovers, this is the greatest of all Mozart's sonatas. Written in the aftermath of his mother's death in Paris (3 July 1778), it brings to his piano sonatas a depth and turbulence of feeling not even hinted at in any of its predecessors. Dramatic and concise, it reaches its highest point of intensity in the middle section of the slow movement, marked *Andante cantabile con espressione*. With its juxtapositions of dynamic extremes, its anguished leaps in the right hand, its stabbing discords, and its plumbing of what was then the piano's lowest register, this music has an emotional immediacy that can make the listener feel almost intrusive. In its combination of grief and anger it conforms to the normal pattern of bereavement. Approached historically, it is significant for Mozart's characteristic use of all the most recent innovations in the piano's capacities (the instrument was evolving at an unprecedented rate) and for being an unsparing attack on the lightweight *galant* ideal. To that extent, it may also be seen as a symbolic assault on his father and all that he represented.

[12] Mass in C minor, K.427 'Great'. **Kyrie**

Eric Blom's theory about Mozart and the minor mode applies here, as in the G minor Symphony and the A minor Sonata. These are all profoundly emotional declarations of independence, each involving the shedding of a repression. Not only is this mass (never completed) a celebration of Mozart's marriage, it was first performed in Salzburg, marking Constanze's introduction to her hostile father- and sister-in-law. Surpassing in grandeur and mastery anything written for the church during his years of servitude to the Archbishop, the work and the choice of venue for its premiere amounted to a massive rebuke to his native city. Magnificently scored for two pairs each of oboes, bassoons, horns, trumpets and timpani, three trombones, string orchestra and organ, the Mass reflects Mozart's immersion in the (for him) newly discovered masterworks of Handel and J.S. Bach. The Italianate, 'operatic' 'Christe eleison' in the opening Kyrie, heard here, may have been sung by Constanze herself. It may have been written expressly to annoy the austere Colloredo, who deplored such things.

Annotations of CD Tracks: CD 2

1. The Abduction from the Seraglio, K.384. **Overture**

Die Entführung aus dem Serail ('The Abduction from the Seraglio'), produced in Vienna in the summer of 1782, marked Mozart's first major theatrical success in the Austrian capital. In essence a light-hearted 'rescue' opera, but leavened with moments of deep seriousness as well, the work capitalises on the contemporary fashion for Turkish subjects and styles. The Overture sets the tone with a suitably 'Turkish' orchestra, featuring the obligatory cymbals, triangle, piccolo and bass drum (the character-giving staples of the Turkish military band) along with oboes, clarinets, horns, trumpets, timpani and strings. An unexpected feature is the slow central section, which introduces a serious element – a tip-off to the audience that the rowdy razzmatazz of the opening section is only part of the story about to unfold.

2. Serenade in B flat for 13 Wind Instruments, K.36. **Romanze: Adagio**

In March 1784 a Viennese newspaper announced that a benefit concert for Mozart's friend and skittles companion, the clarinettist Anton Stadler, would contain 'a large wind work of a very special kind by Herr Mozart'. The work in question was the Serenade in B flat, K.361, by common consent the finest work ever written for wind ensemble. No doubt because of the serenade's length, only four of its seven movements were performed at Stadler's concert. Interestingly, the sixth movement is almost note-for-note the same as the second movement of his Flute Quartet in C, written some time earlier. Bach and Handel often recycled their own works, Mozart hardly ever. That he should do so in a work of this scale and importance is surprising.

3. Horn Concerto No. 1 in D, K.412. **Rondo: Allegro**

Long numbered as the first of Mozart's four horn concertos, this is in fact the last, composed in 1791 and not completely finished. Because of their relative brevity, easy-going melodic appeal and healthy, outdoorsy character, all four of Mozart's horn concertos have been very popular ever since Dennis Brain's famous 1953 recording with Herbert von Karajan. They are almost invariably recorded as a set, though they were not designed as such. The movement heard here is that annotated by Mozart in terms of a sexual encounter (see p. 120). Listeners bent on identifying the connection between Mozart's manically raunchy commentary and the music should resign themselves to a long and probably fruitless search.

4 String Quartet in C, K.465 'Dissonance'. **Movement 1: Adagio – Allegro**

This prophetic work derives its nickname from the slow introduction to its first movement. Nothing in Mozart's output generated more controversy in his lifetime than these twenty-two mesmerising bars. To one critic, they were merely 'much too highly spiced'. The musical amateur Prince Grassalkowics, by contrast, flew into such a rage over the 'hideous stuff' that he tore up the parts on the spot. The score was returned from Italy to the publisher Artaria as being so obviously full of mistakes that it was impossible to play from it. Almost as noteworthy as the dissonant introduction, however, was its apparent irrelevance to the movement which follows. Even today, it remains for many an impenetrable enigma. The solution, as to many other musical riddles, is not to seek the composer's intentions (this is something we can never know for sure) but to consider the *effect* of what he wrote. This quartet is the climax of the six that Mozart dedicated to Haydn, whose example inspired them. They represented a major learning experience for him, not least where large-scale structure is concerned. At the highest level, the six quartets represent one great 'superwork'. If this is to be perceived, something must set this final quartet off from its five siblings and establish its climactic role. What this enigmatic *Adagio* introduction does is to create an atmosphere of fathomless mystery. The sense of suspense mounts with every bar, focusing the listener's imagination ever more intently on what is to follow. When the release comes and the main *Allegro* gets underway, the effect is one of catharsis. Here, as ever, Mozart was a supreme dramatist.

5 Piano Concerto No. 20 in D minor, K.466. **Finale: Allegro assai**

With the D minor Concerto, Mozart began to lose his audience. Accustomed to a world of *galant* pleasantries, the Viennese – at least a significant portion of them – were disconcerted by the turbulence and the haunting anxiety in this epoch-making masterpiece. This is Mozart's first concerto in the minor mode and a major turning point in his career.

It would be a simplistic exaggeration to say that with this work the Romantic era began. But it was this concerto above all which fired the nineteenth-century imagination, none more so than Beethoven's. Indeed, his cadenzas for the first and last movements have become almost as famous as the work itself.

6 The Marriage of Figaro, K.492. **Act III, No. 19: Sestetto 'Riconosci in questo amplesso'**

Nothing better demonstrates Mozart's subtlety and virtuosity as a psychological dramatist than this astonishing vocal sextet. The complexities of the plot are too great to summarise briefly in explanation of this unique ensemble. Suffice it to say that it brings together six characters, keeps them *in* character throughout, and even manages to develop them in the process. One of the marvels of the sextet is the marvel of music itself: in what other medium could six different voices, saying six different things, in six different moods, from six different vantage points, speak at once and produce anything but chaos? Miraculously, Mozart actually advances the drama without any cost to the beauty of the music.

7 Don Giovanni, K.527. **Overture**

Just as the D minor Concerto was *the* Mozart concerto of choice for the Romantics of the nineteenth century, so *Don Giovanni* (also based in D minor) was the quintessential Mozart opera. By this time, the Mozartian overture was very much more than a crowd-settling curtain-raiser; more, too, than a loose pot-pourri of the main themes to be encountered in the opera proper. Though written down at the last moment, the Overture to *Don Giovanni* is a superbly integrated tone poem, more like a prophecy than a preview. Its atmosphere holds one with the grip of an emotional vice, doom-laden yet thrilling, diabolical yet sublime, comic yet tragic; and as in many of Mozart's late masterpieces, his use of chromaticism is spine-tingling.

8 Symphony No. 40 in G minor, K.550. **Movement 3: Menuetto – Trio**

Another favourite with the Romantics, indeed their favourite eighteenth-century symphony from any source, this is only the second of Mozart's symphonies to be cast in the minor mode. The first, also in G minor, was No. 25, K.183 (see CD 1, track 6). G minor was clearly a dark, essentially tragic key for Mozart. His only other works in this key – all of them significant – are the String Quintet, K.516, the Piano Quartet No. 1, K.478, and the Sonata Movement, K.312 for piano. The particular range of moods they express is not found in any of his works in other keys. The most famous movement of the Symphony No. 40 is the first, not least (sadly) thanks to countless digital alarm clocks and mobile phones which have dulled people's sensibilities when they come to hear the real thing. In some ways the most striking movement is the third, a Minuet and Trio. Traditionally the Minuet is the lightest movement in a symphonic context. Here, by contrast, we come close to the kind of fist-shaking defiance associated with Beethoven (whose fist-shaking key tended to be C minor). In the context of Mozart's total symphonic output, the last three, evidently conceived as a trilogy, are surrounded by mystery. No one knows what prompted their composition in the summer of 1788, or whether they were even performed in Mozart's lifetime. Given that he was then only thirty-two and in excellent health, it seems inconceivable that he envisaged them as his symphonic swan song.

9 Così fan tutte, K.588. **Act I, Scene 2: Terzettino 'Soave sia il vento'**

Così fan tutte has been described by one eminent Mozartian, Professor Edward J. Dent, as 'the most exquisite work of art among Mozart's operas', and many agree with this judgement. To anyone familiar with the plot alone, this might seem surprising. Derided both for its sheer silliness and its supposed immorality, it revolves around a far-fetched test by two young officers of their respective mistresses' fidelity. Pretending to be called away on active service, they reappear disguised, improbably, as Albanians, each wooing the lover of the other. The exquisiteness of the music, however, is less noteworthy from a purely historical point of view, than the domination of the opera by inspired and often prolonged ensembles, rather than the traditional sequence of arias and duets (not that *Così* lacks either). Perhaps the most ravishing number in the whole opera is the trio in Act I where the duped young women, joined by their cynical friend Don Alfonso, wish the departing officers Godspeed: 'May the winds blow gently and the waves be calm, may every element look kindly on all our desires.'

[10] The Magic Flute, K.620. **Act II, No. 14: Aria 'Der Hölle Rache'**

In the history of opera there is no one to surpass Mozart as a master of ensemble. But he was equally a master of the virtuosic showstopper. Nothing more sensationally puts him at the top of the tree in that department than the Queen of the Night's famous tirade in Act II of *The Magic Flute*. In a coloratura aria renowned for its fearsome demands on the very top of the soprano's range, the Queen sings of the vengeance of hell that is in her heart.

[11] Clarinet Concerto in A, K.622. **Movement 2: Adagio**

This sublime concerto was Mozart's last major completed work. Like the equally great Clarinet Quintet, the Clarinet Trio, and the obbligatos for the clarinet and basset-horn in his final opera *La clemenza di Tito*, it was composed for Anton Stadler, perhaps the greatest clarinettist of the day. As it happens, neither the Concerto nor the Quintet was written for the instrument we know today, but rather for the deeper-toned 'basset-clarinet', a close relation (not to be confused with either the basset-horn or the bass clarinet), designed by Stadler himself. The exquisite slow movement, with its 'autumnal' harmonic colouring, may give us some idea of how Mozart might have developed had he lived. In any case, he demonstrates his absolute oneness with the instrument and its capacities, and leaves us wondering, 'After this, can we even *think* of asking anything more?'

[12] Requiem in D minor, K.626. **Kyrie**

The Kyrie is the second movement of the Requiem, and the first of those requiring a helping hand after Mozart's death. But the basics were there. The vocal parts were complete, so was the bass line, complete with figures to indicate how the harmony should be filled out. The orchestral parts, too, were sketched in here and there, so its completion was not a major challenge. Though undeniably Mozartian, this Kyrie reflects the profound influence of Handel on Mozart's musical thinking. Indeed listeners familiar with *Messiah* may notice a striking resemblance between the opening subject of this magnificent double fugue and Handel's great chorus 'And with His Stripes we are Healed'. But if it looks back it also seems to look forward, to Beethoven, who once famously (and exceptionally) said of Handel, 'To *him* I bend the knee.' This music, with its astounding vigour and immensity of vision, defies us to believe that its composer's life was soon to be extinguished. A Requiem this may be; but it is perhaps the most life-enhancing example of a mass for the dead in the history of music.

13 Piano Concerto No. 25 in C, K.503. **Finale: Allegretto.**

There is no evidence that he thought much about these things, but it is doubtful that Mozart would be surprised that his music has long since taken its place at the centre of western musical culture – and more than that, in the hearts of music lovers all over the world. It might be appropriate, chronologically, to end his story with the Requiem. But while Mozart reflected every aspect of human experience, he was also in many ways the most Utopian composer who ever lived. Having embraced reality, his music almost always ends with an affirmation of harmony in every sense. Tensions are released; differences have been resolved. No matter what has come before, he leaves us in an ideal world of beauty and grace. Nowhere is this truer than in his piano concertos; and nowhere in his piano concertos is this truer than in the finale to K.503.

Index